PSYCHOLOGY OF TECHNOLOGY

Where human psychology meets the digital frontier

Hal F Gottfried

Amazon

This book is dedicated to Heather, my love. Your boundless patience, steadfast belief, and the comforting rhythm of pancakes and coffee made this journey possible. Without your love and encouragement, it simply wouldn't exist.

To my extraordinary friends and family, your unwavering support fueled my every step. Thank you for believing in me.

To Joel, your invaluable feedback and caffeinated collaboration were essential.

And to Luis and Skye, your wonderful dinners, stimulating conversations, and unwavering dedication to good have been a constant inspiration.

To my wonderful in-laws, thank you for welcoming me into your family with open arms and for trusting me with your beautiful daughter. Your kindness and support have meant the world to me.

And to my father, whose love and guidance over the years made me who I am today.

This book is a testament to the love and support I've been so fortunate to receive.

CONTENTS

INTRODUCTION

L et's be honest, we're drowning in technology. From the moment that first notification buzzes us awake to the blue light keeping us up at night, our lives are tangled up with screens and apps. This book goes beyond a typical analysis of technology's impact; it explores the intricate ways it influences our thoughts, emotions, and connections with others. Think of it as a journey into the human heart of our digital age.

We'll explore how those clever algorithms subtly nudge our decisions, how social media can hook us like a fishing line, and how the constant pinging and buzzing chip away at our attention and peace of mind. We'll talk about the strange, sometimes wonderful, sometimes terrifying world of online identities, the overwhelming flood of information, and the double-edged sword of technology—its power to both heal and harm. This isn't about throwing our phones into the ocean and living off-grid (though, hey, no judgment if you want to!). It's about building a healthier relationship with the technology that's woven into the fabric of our lives. It's about understanding how it works, both the good and the bad, so we can make conscious choices, not just react to the next notification. We'll figure out how to navigate this wild digital landscape with more awareness and intention, building a life that's empowering and fulfilling, even in a world increasingly defined by screens. Let's dive in. The chapters ahead will unpack all this, giving you the tools you need to take charge of your digital life.

CHAPTER 1: THE DIGITAL LANDSCAPE: OUR INCREASINGLY INTERTWINED LIVES

THE UBIQUITY OF TECHNOLOGY AND ITS INFILTRATION INTO DAILY LIFE

Technology isn't just something we use anymore - it's become part of who we are. I still remember when getting my first smartphone felt like a luxury, not a necessity. Now? It's the first thing I check in the morning and the last thing I see at night. And I bet it's the same for you.

Your phone isn't just a device; it's become this weird extension of yourself. Think about it - it's your camera, your map, your social life, your entertainment, your work email... all crammed into that little rectangle that follows you everywhere. Super convenient? For sure. But man, that convenience comes with baggage we rarely unpack and examine.

Remember those days when leaving the office meant you were actually DONE with work? Seems almost quaint now. These days, emails and notifications chase us home, to dinner, even to bed. The line separating "work hours" from "your time" hasn't just gotten blurry - it's practically gone. We've somehow stumbled into creating this world where being unreachable for even an hour makes you feel weirdly guilty or anxious.

Our relationships look different too. We build these carefully curated online versions of ourselves through filtered photos and highlight-reel posts. We maintain friendships with quick likes and emoji comments. I was at dinner with friends last week and realized at one point that all five of us were checking our phones instead of talking to each other. When was the last time you made it through a meal without someone (maybe you?) glancing down at a notification?

Even the way we relax has been hijacked. Instead of doing nothing - which used to be a perfectly acceptable way to spend time - we've got Netflix queues that never end and games designed to keep us playing for hours. These digital worlds can be amazing for connecting with others, but they can also suck us in until we forget to look up.

Time and space feel different now too. I can video chat with friends across the globe as easily as I can text my neighbor. That's incredible! But this constant connection creates this bizarre time crunch.

We're constantly multitasking, always half-listening to something else, always slightly distracted by the possibility of something more important happening elsewhere.

UNDERSTANDING THE PSYCHOLOGICAL IMPACT OF TECHNOLOGY

If we want to really get how technology affects us, we've gotta move past just labeling it "good" or "bad." It's not passive - it actively rewires how we think, feel, and behave. And this impact hits everyone differently based on how they use tech, their personality, and which specific technologies they interact with.

Think about your brain on a typical online day. Information overload is real - your brain wasn't built to process this much input. I notice it myself after heavy social media sessions - trying to focus on writing or reading afterward feels like swimming through mud. There's research backing this up too - excessive screen time actually shrinks your working memory capacity, making complex thinking harder.

I've started calling this state "continuous partial attention" - that feeling where you're never 100% focused on anything because you're constantly bouncing between tasks and inputs. Part of your brain stays on high alert, waiting for the next ping, the next update, the next whatever. It's exhausting! And it completely changes how we process information and experience the world.

The emotional stuff is just as complicated. Social media can be genuinely amazing for finding your people - especially if you're someone with niche interests or living in a small town. But these same platforms can trigger some pretty dark feelings - jealousy when scrolling through vacation photos, anxiety about missing out, or feeling inadequate compared to someone's highlight reel.

Be honest - have you ever posted something and then kept checking back every few minutes to see who liked it? I definitely have. That's not just random behavior - it's a programmed response to those variable reward systems built into these platforms. We're seeking validation, and the unpredictable timing of when (or if) that validation comes keeps us checking obsessively.

The changes to our social behavior might be the most obvious shift. We can connect with people worldwide in ways that would've seemed magical twenty years ago. But these connections often lack depth. A like button doesn't require the emotional investment of a real conversation. And people say stuff online they'd never dream of saying to someone's face - the worst of human behavior often flourishes behind avatars and usernames.

Our physical health takes a hit too. Sitting around staring at screens for hours isn't exactly what bodies evolved to do. The blue light messes with sleep. That hunched-over "phone posture" causes neck problems I never had before smartphones existed.

But look, technology isn't all downsides. Educational resources that were once limited to elite universities are now available to anyone with internet access. Health apps have gotten people moving who never would've joined a gym. Telemedicine reaches people in remote areas who couldn't access care before. And for people with disabilities, new technologies have created independence that wasn't possible previously.

What makes the difference between tech that helps versus tech that harms? It's this messy mix of design choices, personal usage patterns, and individual resilience. The exact same Instagram account that connects one person to a supportive community might send another into a spiral of social comparison and anxiety. Context matters enormously.

THE NEUROSCIENCE OF TECHNOLOGY ENGAGEMENT

Ever wonder why it's so damn hard to put down your phone? There's some fascinating brain stuff happening behind the scenes. It's actually the same system that makes chocolate delicious and new love feel intoxicating - your brain's reward pathway.

Here's how the whole thing works: Every time your phone pings with a notification, you get a tiny hit of dopamine in your brain. But here's the kicker - it's not actually the notification itself that's addictive. It's the ANTICIPATION of what that notification might be. Who liked your post? Did your crush finally respond? Is there breaking news? This unpredictability creates this powerful loop that keeps you coming back for more.

It works exactly like slot machines (which is no accident). The unpredictable nature of rewards - sometimes you get something great, sometimes nothing - makes it incredibly difficult to walk away. App designers aren't dumb - they've built interfaces specifically designed to deliver these variable rewards at precisely the right intervals to keep you engaged just a bit longer... and then a bit longer still.

Next time you're mindlessly scrolling, try to notice the design tricks triggering your reward system. The red notification dots. The pull-to-refresh feature that works just like pulling a slot machine lever. The autoplay that keeps serving up videos without you having to decide to continue. None of these are accidental - they're engineered specifically to hook into your brain's reward mechanisms.

The problem isn't that rewards exist - our brains evolved this dopamine system for good reasons. It helps us learn what benefits us and motivates us to repeat rewarding behaviors. The issue is that technology creates this shortcut to trigger rewards without any corresponding real-world benefits. Your brain registers a like on social media as meaningful social connection, even when that "connection" is completely superficial.

Over time, this constant artificial stimulation messes with your natural reward cycle. Things that used to bring pleasure - reading a book, taking a walk, having a face-to-face conversation - might seem boring because they don't deliver that immediate dopamine hit. I've caught myself reaching for my phone during these activities, seeking that quick boost of stimulation.

This affects everyone differently. Some people develop genuinely addictive relationships with their devices, complete with withdrawal symptoms when separated from them. Others maintain a healthier relationship but still feel that pull. Age makes a huge difference too - developing brains are especially vulnerable to these manipulation techniques, which explains the alarming mental health trends we're seeing in teenagers as social media use increases.

The big-picture implications are pretty profound when you step back and think about it. We've created a world where billions of people spend hours every day on platforms specifically designed to maximize engagement through these neurological mechanisms. This isn't just changing individual well-being - it's reshaping social norms, attention spans, and how we perceive reality itself.

TECHNOLOGY AND THE TRANSFORMATION

OF HUMAN RELATIONSHIPS

I think technology's biggest impact might be on our relationships. The ways we meet people, connect with them, communicate, and build intimacy have completely transformed - sometimes for better, sometimes for worse.

Long-distance relationships are a perfect example of technology's double-edged sword. Before video calls and instant messaging, maintaining a connection across distance was crazy difficult and expensive. I remember making carefully planned, timed international calls in the 90s, watching the minutes tick by on the phone bill. Now? Partners separated by oceans can share daily moments, see each other's faces, and maintain real intimacy in ways that were impossible before. Families spread across continents can celebrate holidays together virtually. Friends can work on projects together despite living in different time zones.

But here's the weird paradox - this ease of digital connection can actually make meaningful conversation harder. Have you noticed how tough it is to have a deep, focused discussion when everyone's phones are sitting on the table? The mere possibility of interruption creates what researchers call "attention residue" - part of your brain stays on standby for the next notification, even when your phone is face-down or on silent.

The pressure to be constantly available is flat-out exhausting. We've created this unspoken expectation of immediate response. That text you haven't answered in a few hours? That email sitting in your inbox since yesterday? They create this background anxiety that simply wasn't part of human experience until very recently. The need to always be "on" leaves many of us feeling resentful and drained, with less energy for genuine connection.

Digital platforms also miss so many of the subtle cues that make up human communication. Body language, tone of voice, the tiny expressions that flash across someone's face - these are mostly lost in text and even partly absent in video calls. We're trying to communicate with a significant chunk of our natural social tools missing. No wonder misunderstandings happen so frequently online.

Social media has created perhaps the most dramatic shift in relationship dynamics. These platforms make connection easier but simultaneously fuel unhealthy comparison. We see these carefully curated personas - just vacation highlights, career wins, and perfectly lit family moments - and measure our own messy, complex lives against this impossible standard.

For teenagers still figuring out who they are, this constant exposure to edited, idealized representations is particularly brutal. Imagine navigating the already rocky terrain of adolescence while constantly bombarded with seemingly perfect lives of peers and influencers. Is it any surprise anxiety and depression have skyrocketed in this age group?

Dating has transformed in similarly complex ways. The expanded opportunities to meet compatible partners can be incredibly liberating, especially for people with specific interests or those in remote areas. But the seemingly endless options can also create this "grass is always greener" mentality. People become less willing to work through normal relationship challenges, knowing another swipe might bring someone "better" or easier.

Even family dynamics have shifted significantly. Technology enables more frequent communication between family members but can diminish the quality of time together. How many family dinners have you witnessed where multiple people are checking phones instead of talking to each other? Parents struggle with the impossible task of modeling healthy technology use while also making sure their kids get enough attention and engagement.

Our core challenge is finding balance - harnessing technology's ability to enhance relationships while minimizing its tendency to isolate, distract, and ultimately degrade the depth of our connections. This isn't about rejecting technology - it's about creating a tech ecosystem that strengthens rather than weakens the authentic human connections that form the foundation of healthy societies.

Moving forward means making conscious choices

about when, how, and why we use technology in our relationships. It means sometimes deliberately putting devices away so we can be truly present with the people physically around us. It means recognizing when a text message isn't enough and picking up the phone or meeting in person instead. Most importantly, it means reclaiming our agency in these choices rather than passively following patterns established by platforms designed primarily to capture our attention rather than improve our relationships.

This battle for our attention sits at the heart of our technological challenge. When we struggle to be present in our relationships, we're encountering just one symptom of a much larger issue: the attention economy that has transformed our cognitive lives. To navigate technology's influence on our relationships, we must first understand how it systematically captures, fragments, and monetizes our most precious resource—our attention itself. This next chapter explores how our digital environment has fundamentally altered our ability to focus, process information, and engage in deep thinking, creating a new mental landscape we all must learn to navigate.

CHAPTER 2: THE ATTENTION ECONOMY: FRAGMENTED FOCUS AND COGNITIVE OVERLOAD

THE IMPACT OF TECHNOLOGY ON ATTENTION SPANS

Ever caught yourself opening Instagram when you actually meant to check your email? Or realized you've read the same paragraph three times because your mind kept wandering to that notification that just buzzed in your pocket? Don't worry—you're not alone, and honestly, it's not entirely your fault.

Many of us have experienced sitting down to write a simple email only to find ourselves, 45 minutes later, deep in a YouTube rabbit hole watching something completely unrelated. How does this happen?

Through the invisible pull of a digital environment designed to fragment our attention.

The constant barrage of notifications, endless stream of content, and our habit of bouncing between tasks have literally rewired how our brains function. We're experiencing a fundamental shift in our most basic cognitive ability: attention itself.

For centuries, we've understood attention as a spotlight that illuminates what matters while keeping distractions in the shadows. This ability to focus on relevant information while filtering out noise is what lets you learn, make decisions, and solve problems. But our digital environment has introduced an unprecedented level of distraction that challenges this core function.

The science is pretty clear on this. Brain imaging studies show distinct changes in people who frequently multitask and heavily use social media. Your prefrontal cortex—basically your brain's command center for focused attention, working memory, and impulse control—shows reduced activity. It's like your brain's filtering system is being gradually worn down by constant digital stimulation.

You can probably see the consequences in your own life. That report that once took you two hours now takes four, with several social media breaks in between. The novel you used to lose yourself in now requires tremendous effort to stay engaged past a few pages. Even conversations become challenging to sustain when phones are present. Sound familiar?

Linda Stone, a former Apple and Microsoft executive, coined the perfect term for this new state of mind: "continuous partial attention." Unlike traditional multitasking where you switch between tasks, continuous partial attention involves constantly dividing your awareness across multiple information streams simultaneously. You're on a video call, but also monitoring email notifications, checking text messages, and keeping an eye on breaking news—never fully present anywhere.

This state might feel productive—hey, you're doing so many things at once!—but the research tells a different story. Each attention switch comes with a cognitive cost. Your brain needs time to disengage from one task, recalibrate, and engage with another. These transition costs add up, reducing overall efficiency and increasing errors. The result? A shallower understanding of everything you engage with and poorer retention of information.

The impact goes far beyond productivity. The erosion of sustained attention undermines your capacity for the deep thinking that defines us as humans. Critical analysis, creative problem-solving, and meaningful connection all require sustained focus. When you can't maintain attention, you become more susceptible to superficial arguments and manipulative content, lacking the mental resources to evaluate complex issues thoughtfully.

Have you noticed how different types of attention suffer in different ways? Sustained attention—your ability to focus on one task for an extended period—takes the biggest hit. Reading a book or writing an essay becomes increasingly difficult amid the constant pull of digital distractions. Selective attention—your ability to filter irrelevant information—also weakens as you're bombarded with an endless stream of content designed to capture your interest.

The biggest culprits? Social media platforms and content streaming services. These aren't just entertainment tools—they're sophisticated engagement machines designed to maximize the time you spend consuming content. Their algorithms learn exactly what keeps you scrolling, clicking, and watching, creating a personalized rabbit hole of endless content. The variable reward schedules (sometimes you see something amazing, sometimes not) exploit the same psychological principles that make slot machines addictive.

But technology isn't inherently destructive to attention. Some digital tools actually help us manage focus better. Meditation and mindfulness apps can train attention. Time management software and website blockers can limit distractions. The same technological ingenuity that created these attention challenges can also help solve them.

The path forward lies in developing a more

intentional relationship with your devices. This means setting boundaries around screen time, using tools to manage digital distractions, and deliberately engaging in activities that build sustained attention. It means recognizing when platforms are designed to hijack your attention and consciously resisting these manipulations.

The goal isn't to eliminate technology from your life—that's neither realistic nor desirable. It's about reclaiming your autonomy in how you engage with it. We need to design and use technology in ways that enhance rather than undermine our uniquely human cognitive abilities, creating a digital environment that serves our deeper purposes rather than distracting us from them.

MULTITASKING AND ITS COGNITIVE COSTS: THE ILLUSION OF EFFICIENCY

"I'm an excellent multitasker!"

How many times have you heard someone brag about this supposed skill? Maybe you've said it yourself. Many people wear their ability to juggle multiple tasks like a badge of honor. We pride ourselves on answering emails while on Zoom calls, checking social media while writing reports, or responding to texts while in meetings. This frantic activity feels productive—even necessary in our fast-paced world.

But here's the uncomfortable truth: multitasking is a

myth. What you're actually doing is task-switching, and it's costing you dearly in terms of efficiency, accuracy, and mental energy.

Your brain simply isn't wired to process multiple complex tasks simultaneously. When you think you're multitasking, you're actually rapidly shifting your attention between different activities. This constant switching comes with a significant cognitive penalty. Each transition requires your brain to disengage from one task, recalibrate its resources, and engage with another. These "switching costs" accumulate, resulting in reduced performance across all the tasks you're juggling.

Think of it like repeatedly restarting your computer instead of letting it run one program efficiently. Your mental processing slows down, and you become more vulnerable to errors and oversights. The cognitive toll isn't minor—research by Sanbonmatsu et al. (2013) suggests that task-switching can substantially reduce productivity, with some studies indicating reductions of up to 40% in efficiency.

This is a lesson many of us learn the hard way. Anyone who has tried to finish an important presentation while simultaneously responding to "urgent" emails knows how a two-hour task can stretch into an entire afternoon, often with mistakes that require additional time to fix.

Neuroscience gives us a clear picture of what's happening. Research on multitasking using neuroimaging techniques has shown that the prefrontal cortex—the brain region responsible for executive functions like attention regulation and working memory—becomes overloaded during task-switching (Wilmer et al., 2017). This overload results in reduced neural activity, impairing your ability to focus, filter distractions, and organize tasks effectively.

Perhaps most significantly, multitasking prevents you from achieving a state of "flow"—that deeply satisfying condition of complete absorption in a challenging but manageable task. During flow, your brain operates with remarkable efficiency, allowing you to process information accurately and creatively while experiencing a sense of timelessness and intrinsic reward. But the fragmented attention caused by constant task-switching makes flow impossible to achieve, robbing you of both peak performance and deep satisfaction in your work.

The behavioral consequences extend beyond simple inefficiency. Chronic multitaskers show poorer performance on tasks requiring sustained attention, memory, and cognitive control. They make more errors, take longer to complete tasks, and report higher levels of stress and frustration. Over time, these individuals often develop diminished attention spans and increased distractibility even when they're trying to focus on a single task. The habit of constant switching actually reshapes your attentional capabilities.

Here's the irony: those who perceive themselves as excellent multitaskers are typically the worst performers in research studies. The confidence in their multitasking ability correlates with poorer executive control and a reduced capacity to filter out irrelevant information. This creates a dangerous cycle —the people most likely to multitask are the ones most vulnerable to its negative effects.

Our digital environment exacerbates these challenges. The constant stream of notifications, emails, and social media updates creates a perfect storm for task-switching, fragmenting your attention and diminishing your cognitive abilities. Digital platforms are explicitly designed to maximize engagement, capitalizing on your natural desire for novelty and immediate gratification. Each notification activates your orienting response—an evolutionarily adaptive reaction that draws your attention to potential threats or rewards in your environment. But in our digital world, these "threats" and "rewards" are largely manufactured to keep you engaged with platforms rather than signaling genuinely important information.

Have you ever noticed how just having your phone visible on your desk—even if it's face down and silent—seems to drain some of your mental energy? Research confirms this intuition. The mere presence of your phone diverts some of your attentional resources to monitoring it, even when you're consciously trying to ignore it.

The addictive nature of many digital technologies creates a particularly vicious cycle: you constantly switch between tasks, experience reduced cognitive performance, yet feel compelled to maintain the habit regardless. The dopamine hits associated with checking notifications or receiving social media engagement can become powerful reinforcers, driving individuals to engage with these platforms even when they are aware of the negative consequences.

The fear of missing out (FOMO), amplified by social media's constant stream of updates and curated highlight reels, contributes to this compulsive behavior. Another important factor is the potential for social isolation and decreased real-world interaction.

Paradoxically, technology also offers potential solutions. Productivity applications, website blockers, and notification management tools can help minimize distractions and encourage focused work. Digital well-being features on smartphones allow you to set limits on app usage and schedule do-not-disturb periods. Mindfulness apps provide structured exercises to develop attentional control and reduce the compulsion to constantly check devices. The key is using these tools intentionally to create environments conducive to focused attention rather than fragmented switching.

Breaking free from the multitasking trap requires a fundamental shift in how you approach your work and technology use. Techniques like time blocking —dedicating specific periods to single tasks without interruption—can dramatically improve productivity and reduce the cognitive load of constant switching. The Pomodoro Technique, with its 25-minute focused work intervals followed by short breaks, provides a structured approach to maintaining concentration while acknowledging your need for periodic mental rest.

Creating physical environments that support focused attention is equally important. Designating a distraction-free workspace, using noise-canceling headphones, and keeping your phone out of sight during concentrated work periods significantly reduces the temptation to multitask. Communicating boundaries to colleagues regarding availability and response times helps manage expectations and reduce the pressure for immediate reactions to non-urgent matters.

The societal implications of chronic multitasking extend far beyond individual productivity. In an increasingly complex world, the ability to engage in deep thinking, critically analyze information, and develop creative solutions is essential. The fragmentation of attention through constant task-switching undermines these capabilities, potentially affecting our collective ability to address complex challenges effectively. When multitasking becomes normalized, we risk creating a culture where superficial engagement with information is standard and deeper analysis is exceptional.

Ready for a small but powerful change? Try this tomorrow: choose one important task, set a timer for 25 minutes, put your phone in another room, and focus solely on that task until the timer rings. Notice how it feels to give something your complete attention, even if just for a short period. This simple practice can be the first step toward reclaiming your cognitive resources.

The path forward requires a reevaluation of your relationship with technology and a commitment to more intentional work practices. By understanding the cognitive costs of multitasking and implementing strategies to promote focused attention, you can reclaim your mental resources and enhance both productivity and well-being. The goal isn't to eliminate technology but to harness its potential to support rather than undermine your cognitive capabilities.

INFORMATION OVERLOAD AND COGNITIVE FATIGUE: DROWNING IN THE DIGITAL DELUGE

Every day, you're bombarded with more information than your ancestors encountered in their entire lifetimes. Think about that for a moment.

Your phone pings with breaking news alerts. Your email inbox fills faster than you can empty it. Your social media feeds update constantly with friends' updates, global events, and trending topics. Add in Slack messages, texts, podcasts, streaming services, and the vast resources of the internet, and you're facing an unprecedented flood of information.

This isn't just overwhelming—it's fundamentally changing how your brain works.

Many of us have experienced spending a morning bouncing between email, news sites, and social media, only to feel mentally exhausted by lunchtime despite having accomplished relatively little. This experience has become so common we barely question it anymore. But this state—what experts call "cognitive fatigue"—isn't just ordinary tiredness.

Your cognitive system wasn't designed for this volume of input. The human brain evolved in an environment where information was scarce and attention-worthy events were rare. Our attentional mechanisms developed to filter relevant information from irrelevant noise, but the sheer quantity of data we now encounter overwhelms these filtering systems. The result is cognitive overload—a state where your brain simply cannot process all the incoming stimuli effectively.

Have you ever felt mentally exhausted after hours of back-to-back video calls or endless social media scrolling? That's cognitive fatigue in action. This isn't ordinary tiredness; it's a state of mental exhaustion that impairs your ability to think clearly, make decisions, and remember important information. When your brain is constantly processing new inputs without adequate recovery time, its resources become depleted. Your working memory capacity decreases, your attention fragments, and your executive function—the control system that manages your cognitive processes—struggles to operate effectively.

Research shows clear connections between information overload and impaired decision-making. When your cognitive resources are depleted, you're more likely to rely on mental shortcuts and heuristics rather than careful analysis. This increases your susceptibility to cognitive biases, leading to impulsive choices and poor judgments. You might find yourself making decisions based on what's immediately available to your mind rather than what's actually most important or relevant.

Ever notice how you tend to make poorer food choices

when mentally exhausted? Or how you're more likely to impulsively buy something online after a long day of information processing? These aren't coincidences —they're direct consequences of cognitive fatigue.

Your memory suffers too. The brain needs time to consolidate new information, transferring it from short-term to long-term memory through a process that requires attention and mental space. When you're constantly processing new inputs, this consolidation process gets interrupted. Information slips away before it can be properly encoded, leaving you struggling to remember important details, recall facts, and retain new knowledge.

The "always-on" culture enabled by technology amplifies these issues. The expectation of immediate responses creates constant pressure, eliminating the natural breaks your brain needs to recover. When was the last time you spent a day completely disconnected from digital communication? For many people, even vacations have become working holidays, with occasional email checks and "just a quick response to this important message."

This constant connectivity leads to a chronic state of alertness that prevents true mental rest. Your brain remains partially activated even during downtime, anticipating the next notification or message that might require your attention. This background vigilance depletes cognitive resources even when you're not actively working, creating a persistent state of mental fatigue that becomes increasingly difficult to overcome.

The societal implications are profound. When information overload becomes the norm, our collective ability to engage in thoughtful discourse diminishes. Complex issues get reduced to simplistic talking points. Nuance disappears in favor of easily digestible content that requires minimal mental effort. This creates fertile ground for misinformation and polarization, as people gravitate toward content that reinforces existing beliefs rather than challenging them to think more deeply.

But there are effective strategies to combat information overload and cognitive fatigue. The first step is recognizing that not all information deserves your attention. Deliberately curating your information diet—choosing high-quality sources, limiting exposure to redundant content, and filtering out low-value inputs—can significantly reduce cognitive load.

Think of information like food. Just as you wouldn't eat everything put in front of you regardless of its nutritional value, you shouldn't consume all available information regardless of its importance or relevance. Being selective about what you allow into your mental space is not ignorance—it's necessary self-preservation in an age of information abundance.

Here are some practical techniques that can help manage information:

- Creating designated times for checking email and messages rather than responding to each notification as it arrives

- Using technology tools to filter content, blocking distracting websites during focused work periods

- Unsubscribing from newsletters and notifications that don't provide significant value

- Implementing a "one in, one out" policy for news sources and social media accounts

- Practicing regular digital detoxes—periods of complete disconnection from digital devices

Many people who have experimented with checking email just three times daily—morning, noon, and late afternoon—report that their initial anxiety ("What if I miss something urgent?") quickly gives way to a profound sense of mental spaciousness. Despite the reduced frequency of checks, they handle all important messages effectively while reclaiming hours of focused time and significantly reducing mental fatigue.

Mindfulness practices can strengthen your ability to maintain focus amid distractions. Regular meditation enhances attentional control, improves focus, and reduces reactivity to interruptions. Even brief mindfulness exercises throughout the day can help reset your attention and clear mental space. Physical activity, adequate sleep, and time in nature are equally important, providing the cognitive recovery needed to maintain mental resilience.

Effective time management techniques can also reduce cognitive load. Breaking tasks into smaller, manageable units prevents the overwhelm that often accompanies complex projects. Prioritizing tasks based on importance rather than urgency helps direct limited cognitive resources to high-value activities. Scheduling dedicated focus blocks—periods of uninterrupted concentration on a single task—can dramatically improve productivity while reducing mental fatigue.

Developing critical thinking skills is essential for navigating the information landscape. Learning to evaluate sources, identify potential biases, and distinguish fact from opinion allows you to process information more efficiently. This discernment reduces the cognitive resources wasted on low-quality or misleading content, allowing you to focus on what's truly valuable.

On a broader level, organizational and societal changes are needed. Workplaces can implement policies that discourage after-hours email and promote recovery periods between intense work sessions. Educational institutions can teach information literacy and cognitive management skills, preparing students for the challenges of the digital information environment. Technology developers can design platforms that respect cognitive limitations rather than exploiting them for engagement.

The future of our cognitive well-being depends on developing a more mindful and intentional relationship with information and technology. This isn't about rejecting the digital world but learning to engage with it in ways that support rather than undermine our cognitive capacities. By adopting strategies that manage information flow, optimize cognitive processing, and prioritize mental restoration, we can navigate the digital deluge without drowning in it.

What's one small step you could take today to reduce your information intake? Perhaps unsubscribing from three newsletters you never read? Or designating a 30-minute period this evening to be completely screen-free? These small actions, when practiced consistently, can significantly enhance your cognitive resilience in our information-saturated world.

The goal is sustainable cognitive performance—maintaining clarity, focus, and mental energy in a world of abundant information. This requires shifting from passive consumption to active curation, from reactive responsiveness to intentional engagement. By reclaiming agency in your relationship with information, you can harness the benefits of the digital age while protecting the cognitive resources that make you uniquely human.

THE RISE OF CONTINUOUS PARTIAL ATTENTION: NEVER FULLY PRESENT ANYWHERE

Have you noticed a subtle but profound shift in how you experience the world? You're physically present in a meeting, but mentally tracking email notifications. You're having dinner with family, but part of your awareness is tuned to the phone in your pocket. You're reading this text, but perhaps already thinking about checking social media when you finish this paragraph.

Welcome to the age of continuous partial attention —a fundamentally new state of consciousness that's become our default mode of existence.

Many of us have experienced this during dinners with friends or family. While engaged in conversation, we catch ourselves periodically glancing at our phones whenever they light up. Later, we realize we can't fully recall parts of the conversation—our divided attention prevented us from being truly present for a gathering we'd been looking forward to.

Unlike traditional multitasking where you switch between distinct activities, continuous partial attention involves dividing your awareness across multiple information streams simultaneously. Your attention is never fully committed to any single focus but constantly scanning for new inputs, updates, and potential demands. It's a persistent, low-level state of alertness that keeps you perpetually monitoring your digital environment while attempting to engage with the physical world.

This isn't just distraction—it's a qualitatively different way of experiencing reality, and it's reshaping our cognitive landscape in profound ways.

The neuroscience behind this phenomenon reveals why it's so compelling and difficult to escape. Each digital notification—every email alert, text message, or social media update—triggers a tiny dopamine release in your brain's reward pathway. This neurotransmitter is associated with pleasure, motivation, and anticipation of reward. The unpredictable timing of these notifications creates a powerful reinforcement schedule, similar to what makes gambling addictive. Your brain becomes conditioned to anticipate the next hit of stimulation, making it increasingly difficult to sustain attention on activities that don't provide this constant reinforcement.

This neurochemical cycle creates a state where your brain is constantly poised for the next input, never fully settling into deep, sustained focus. The prefrontal cortex—responsible for complex cognitive processes like planning, decision-making, and impulse control—becomes overtaxed by the constant demand for attention switching. Neural resources that should be dedicated to the task at hand are instead diverted to this continuous monitoring activity, leaving fewer cognitive resources available for deep thinking.

The consequences are far-reaching. Working memory—your ability to hold and manipulate information in consciousness—suffers significantly. Complex problem-solving becomes more difficult as your cognitive resources are fragmented. Creative thinking, which often requires sustained immersion in a problem space, becomes increasingly rare. The ability to make connections between disparate ideas—a hallmark of innovation—diminishes when attention never remains on one concept long enough to explore it deeply.

Perhaps most concerning is the impact on emotional processing. Emotions require attentional space to be fully experienced and integrated. When your attention is perpetually fragmented, emotional experiences become shallower and less nuanced. Positive emotions aren't savored completely, while negative emotions aren't processed adequately. This creates a troubling disconnect from your emotional landscape, potentially contributing to increased stress, anxiety, and emotional dysregulation.

Have you noticed this in your own emotional experiences? Think about the last time you felt joy or sadness. Were you able to fully immerse yourself in the feeling, or was part of your awareness already drifting toward your devices?

Your relationships suffer as well. Meaningful

connection requires presence—the ability to fully attend to another person, to notice subtle emotional cues, to respond authentically to what's being communicated. When your attention is divided, these elements of connection are compromised. Your conversation partner senses your partial presence, even if they can't articulate exactly what's missing. Trust erodes gradually as these micro-moments of inattention accumulate. The quality of communication deteriorates, leading to misunderstandings, decreased empathy, and a pervasive sense of disconnection.

This state of continuous partial attention isn't simply a personal choice—it's actively cultivated by the design of our digital environment. Social media platforms, news websites, and communication tools are engineered to maximize engagement, often at the expense of sustained attention. Notification systems are deliberately designed to interrupt, creating the sense that you might miss something important if you don't immediately check. The user interfaces employ countless subtle psychological tricks to keep you engaged for as long as possible.

The economic incentives behind these design choices are powerful. In the attention economy, your focus is the product being sold to advertisers. The longer platforms can keep you engaged, the more valuable you become as an advertising target. This creates a fundamental misalignment between what's profitable for technology companies and what's beneficial for your cognitive health and well-being.

This isn't to suggest a conspiracy—most individual designers aren't deliberately trying to harm users. But the cumulative effect of optimization for engagement metrics creates systems that naturally exploit our cognitive vulnerabilities. The result is an environment that makes continuous partial attention the path of least resistance, requiring conscious effort to escape its pull.

Societal norms reinforce this pattern. The expectation of immediate responsiveness to messages creates pressure to remain constantly vigilant. The fear of missing important updates or being perceived as unresponsive adds a layer of social anxiety to the neurochemical drivers of continuous partial attention. Work cultures that equate constant connectivity with commitment and dedication further normalize this fragmented attentional state.

But this situation isn't inevitable or irreversible. While the forces shaping continuous partial attention are powerful, strategic approaches can help reclaim your capacity for focused attention.

Awareness is the essential first step. Simply recognizing when you're in a state of continuous partial attention—noticing the urge to check your phone during a conversation, feeling the pull to monitor email while working on a project—creates the possibility of choice. This metacognitive awareness allows you to intervene in the automatic pattern of divided attention.

Try this simple exercise: For the next hour, each time you reach for your phone or feel the urge to check a notification, pause and ask yourself, "Why am I doing this right now? Is it necessary, or is it just habit?" This brief moment of awareness can interrupt the automatic cycle and give you space to make a more intentional choice.

Mindfulness practices can strengthen your attentional control. Regular meditation trains the brain to notice when attention has wandered and bring it back to a chosen focus. This mental exercise builds the neural pathways associated with sustained attention, making it progressively easier to maintain focus despite distractions. Even brief daily practice can yield significant improvements in attentional stability over time.

Deliberately creating spaces free from digital distraction is equally important. Designating specific times for disconnection—perhaps during meals, before bed, or during focused work periods—allows your brain to experience the deeper engagement that comes with sustained attention. These digital detox periods need not be extended or dramatic; even short breaks from connectivity can help reset attentional patterns and provide cognitive recovery.

Environmental design plays a crucial role as well. Physically separating yourself from devices during important conversations or focused work sessions reduces the temptation for divided attention. Disabling notifications for non-urgent applications eliminates many triggers for attentional shifts. Using specialized tools to block distracting websites or apps during designated focus periods can provide external support for attentional boundaries.

Many people find that keeping their phones in another room during dinner and for the first hour after waking up makes a significant difference. The initial discomfort can be revealing—we often don't realize how habitually we check our devices until we make them unavailable. Within days, many notice more vivid memories of conversations, greater emotional presence, and a surprising sense of relief. These small boundaries create spaces of true attention in the day that become increasingly precious.

In workplace settings, creating cultures that respect focused attention is essential. This might involve establishing communication norms that don't require immediate responses, designating specific times for collaboration versus deep work, and modeling healthy attentional boundaries at the leadership level. Organizations that prioritize sustained focus over constant reactivity often see improvements in both productivity and employee well-being.

The challenge of continuous partial attention isn't merely personal—it's systemic and societal. Addressing it requires changes at multiple levels, from individual practice to organizational policy to technology design. By understanding the cognitive and neurological mechanisms driving this attentional pattern, we can develop more effective strategies for creating environments that support rather than undermine our capacity for sustained focus.

The goal isn't to eliminate all distraction or connectivity. Rather, it's to reclaim agency in how we distribute our attention, making conscious choices about when to connect and when to focus deeply. It's about creating a balanced attentional ecosystem that includes both broad scanning and deep immersion, using each mode appropriately rather than defaulting to perpetual fragmentation.

In this effort, we're not just protecting productivity or performance—we're preserving the quality of human experience itself. The capacity for sustained attention is essential for deep understanding, creative insight, emotional processing, and meaningful connection. These are the elements that make life rich and meaningful. By resisting the pull toward continuous partial attention, we're safeguarding our ability to fully engage with the world and with each other—to be truly present in our own lives.

What might change in your relationships, your work, or your emotional well-being if you could be more fully present? What small step could you take today to create a space of undivided attention in your life?

STRATEGIES FOR ENHANCING COGNITIVE FUNCTION IN THE DIGITAL AGE

Now that we understand the challenges our brains face in the digital environment, let's focus on practical solutions. How can you protect and strengthen your cognitive abilities while still benefiting from technology?

The good news: with intentional practices and environmental design, you can develop a healthier relationship with your digital tools and enhance your mental capabilities.

CULTIVATING MINDFULNESS: TRAINING YOUR ATTENTION MUSCLE

Think of your attention as a muscle that can be strengthened through consistent training. Mindfulness meditation is one of the most effective exercises for this cognitive muscle. It's not about emptying your mind but rather about practicing the skill of noticing when your attention has wandered and gently bringing it back to your chosen focus.

Many people who were initially skeptical about meditation have found that it can make a significant difference in their ability to focus. Starting with just five minutes daily, focusing on your breath and simply noticing when your mind wanders (which happens constantly at first) can begin to build the skill of returning your focus. The practice isn't about preventing distractions but about building the skill of recognizing and redirecting attention. Within weeks, many notice the benefits extending beyond meditation—they can catch themselves earlier when falling into distraction spirals during work.

Start small—even five minutes daily can yield benefits. Focus on your breath, bodily sensations, or environmental sounds. When your mind inevitably wanders (and it will), simply notice the distraction without judgment and return your attention to your chosen anchor. This simple practice strengthens the neural pathways associated with attentional control, making it progressively easier to maintain focus in other contexts.

You don't need to limit mindfulness to formal meditation sessions. Integrate it into everyday activities by bringing full attention to routine tasks. When washing dishes, focus completely on the sensations—the temperature of the water, the feeling of soap, the sound of splashing. When eating, notice the flavors, textures, and aromas of your food rather than scrolling through your phone. When walking, observe your surroundings with curiosity rather than immediately reaching for earbuds.

These mindful moments throughout your day serve as micro-training sessions for your attention, gradually building your capacity for sustained focus even amid digital distractions.

MANAGING INFORMATION INTAKE: CURATING YOUR MENTAL DIET

Just as you wouldn't eat everything put in front of you regardless of its nutritional value, you shouldn't consume all available information regardless of its quality or relevance. Being selective about what you allow into your mental space is essential for cognitive health.

Start by auditing your current information diet. Which news sources, social media accounts, newsletters, and podcasts truly enhance your life? Which create stress, anxiety, or waste your time? Be ruthless in eliminating low-value inputs. Unsubscribe from newsletters that no longer serve you. Mute or unfollow social media accounts that trigger negative emotions or comparison. Consider using news aggregators that highlight truly important stories rather than checking multiple sites throughout the day.

Many people who conduct a "digital decluttering" of their information inputs report an immediate sense of relief. Unsubscribing from unnecessary email newsletters, unfollowing accounts across social platforms, and limiting news checking to morning and evening can make a significant difference. The immediate sense of relief is often surprising—we don't always realize how much background anxiety these constant inputs create. More importantly, this approach allows for deeper thinking about fewer topics, rather than having shallow knowledge about many.

Create designated times for information consumption rather than allowing it to infiltrate your entire day. Perhaps check news in the morning and evening rather than throughout the day. Schedule specific periods for email and message checking rather than responding to each notification as it arrives. This batch processing approach reduces the cognitive cost of constant context switching.

Additionally, consider implementing an "information sabbath"—a regular period (perhaps a day or even just an evening) when you deliberately disconnect from news and social media. This mental space allows for processing and integration of information already consumed rather than constant intake of new stimuli.

TIME MANAGEMENT TECHNIQUES: STRUCTURING FOR FOCUS

How you organize your time can dramatically impact your cognitive performance. Strategic approaches to time management can create the conditions for sustained attention and deep work.

Time blocking—dedicating specific periods to particular tasks or types of work—is particularly effective. Rather than reactively responding to whatever demands your attention, proactively schedule blocks for focused work, communication, creative thinking, and personal activities. During these blocks, eliminate distractions and commit fully to the designated activity.

Does this sound familiar? You sit down to work on an important project, but after ten minutes, you get an email notification, switch to your inbox, respond to a few messages, notice a news headline, click to read the article, remember you need to order something online, and thirty minutes later realize you've barely started your original task. Time blocking creates a structure that prevents these attention slips.

The Pomodoro Technique offers a structured approach to maintaining focus while acknowledging our need for breaks. Work with complete concentration for 25 minutes, then take a short 5-minute break. After four cycles, take a longer break of 15-30 minutes. This rhythm works with your brain's natural attention cycle, allowing for periods of intense focus followed by recovery.

Task batching—grouping similar activities together —reduces the cognitive cost of switching between different types of work. For instance, handle all email correspondence in one session rather than checking messages throughout the day. Process all administrative tasks in a dedicated block rather than interspersing them with creative or analytical work. This approach minimizes context-switching penalties and allows you to gain momentum in each type of activity.

TECHNOLOGY MANAGEMENT: TOOLS TO TAME DISTRACTION

Ironically, some of the best solutions for technology-induced cognitive challenges come from technology itself. Numerous applications and features can help you create a digital environment more conducive to focused attention.

Website and app blockers allow you to temporarily restrict access to distracting sites during designated focus periods. These tools can be configured to block specific websites, entire categories (like social media), or even the internet altogether during scheduled times. Some offer flexible options like allowing 5 minutes of access per hour or requiring you to wait through a delay before accessing blocked sites, creating space for the impulse to check to subside.

Many people find that apps like Freedom, which block distracting websites and apps across all devices simultaneously, can be game-changing for productivity. Setting it to block social media and news sites during morning work hours creates a distraction-free zone that allows completion of important work before the day's interruptions begin.

Notification management is equally important. Most devices now offer do-not-disturb modes, focus modes, or custom notification settings. Take time to configure these thoughtfully, allowing only truly urgent communications to interrupt you during important activities. Consider keeping your phone in do-not-disturb mode by default rather than as an exception, checking it intentionally rather than reactively.

Digital wellbeing features built into smartphones and computers can provide insight into your technology usage patterns and help establish healthier habits. Screen time reports reveal how much time you spend on different applications, while downtime settings can automatically limit access to certain apps after designated usage thresholds or during scheduled periods.

PHYSICAL ENVIRONMENT: DESIGNING FOR COGNITIVE HEALTH

Your physical workspace significantly impacts your

ability to maintain focus. Creating an environment that supports sustained attention can reduce the effort required to resist distraction.

When possible, designate separate spaces for different types of activities. Use a specific location for focused work, ideally free from the devices and reminders associated with other activities. This creates environmental cues that signal to your brain which mode of attention is appropriate.

Keep smartphones out of sight during focused work periods—even having your phone visible on your desk, even if it's face down and silent, can reduce cognitive capacity as part of your attention remains aware of its presence. Consider placing it in another room or inside a drawer during important tasks. You wouldn't believe how something so simple can dramatically improve your concentration. Many people report that keeping their phones in a desk drawer during focused work sessions noticeably increases productivity—not just because they're not checking it, but because the mental awareness of it isn't stealing small bits of attention.

Noise-canceling headphones can create an auditory bubble that shields you from environmental distractions. Some people find that specific types of music or ambient sounds (like rainfall or coffee shop noise) help maintain focus by providing non-distracting background stimulation that masks more disruptive sounds.

Natural elements in your workspace can support cognitive function. Views of nature, indoor plants, and natural light have all been shown to enhance attention and reduce mental fatigue. If possible, position your workspace near a window or incorporate plants and natural materials into your environment. Many people find that even adding just two small plants to a desk area makes a noticeable difference—glancing at them throughout the day provides mini mental refreshment breaks.

Does your workspace support or undermine your attention? Take a moment to scan your environment. What small changes could you make that would reduce visual clutter, minimize distractions, or add elements that support sustained focus?

ORGANIZATIONAL AND CULTURAL CHANGE: CREATING SUPPORTIVE SYSTEMS

Individual strategies, while important, are insufficient without broader systemic support. In workplace contexts, organizational policies and cultural norms can either undermine or enhance cognitive wellness.

Advocate for communication guidelines that respect focus time. This might include designated "quiet hours" when interruptions are minimized, expectations around email response times that don't require constant monitoring, or the use of asynchronous communication methods that allow people to engage at optimal times rather than demanding immediate attention.

Many workplaces have implemented "Focus Fridays" where meetings are discouraged and everyone is expected to respect each other's concentration time. The impact is often immediate—complex projects that had been stalling begin moving forward, and people report feeling less frazzled at week's end. This simple policy change creates breathing room for deep work in an otherwise meeting-heavy culture.

Promote meeting practices that respect cognitive limitations. This includes clear agendas, time boundaries, and thoughtful consideration of which discussions truly require synchronous participation. Not every exchange needs to be a meeting—many can be handled more efficiently through collaborative documents or messaging platforms, reducing the interruptions that fragment attention.

Encourage work cultures that value deep work alongside connectivity. This means recognizing that constant availability often comes at the expense of high-quality thinking and creative problem-solving. Organizations that create space for uninterrupted focus often see improvements in both innovation and execution.

EDUCATION AND AWARENESS: BUILDING COGNITIVE RESILIENCE

Long-term cognitive health in the digital age requires broader educational initiatives that equip people with the knowledge and skills to navigate an attention-hostile environment.

Schools should integrate attention management and digital literacy into their curricula, teaching students not just how to use technology but how to use it mindfully. Understanding the cognitive impacts of different digital behaviors allows young people to make more informed choices about their technology use.

Workplace training programs should address cognitive wellness alongside other professional development topics. This includes practical strategies for managing digital distraction, organizing information effectively, and structuring work to maximize cognitive performance.

Public awareness campaigns can help normalize healthy digital boundaries and counter the cultural assumption that constant connectivity equals productivity or dedication. By shifting social norms around technology use, we can create environments more supportive of cognitive health.

The path to enhanced cognitive function in the digital age isn't about rejecting technology but developing a more intentional relationship with it. By implementing these multifaceted strategies—from mindfulness practices and information curation to environmental design and systemic change—we can protect and strengthen our cognitive capabilities while still benefiting from digital tools.

Many people find that combining several of these approaches creates a powerful synergy. For instance, starting the day with a brief meditation, followed by 90 minutes of distraction-free focus time (phone away, notifications off), and batching email checks to three designated times daily has transformed productivity and significantly reduced stress levels for countless professionals. The key is consistency —these practices become truly effective once they become habits rather than occasional efforts.

This isn't a one-time fix but an ongoing practice of awareness and adjustment. The digital landscape continues to evolve, presenting new cognitive challenges that require adaptive strategies. By approaching this evolution mindfully, we can create a future where technology enhances rather than diminishes our uniquely human cognitive abilities— a future where we harness digital tools in service of deeper thinking, more meaningful connection, and greater well-being.

What one strategy from this section resonates most with you? Could you implement it tomorrow as a small experiment in reclaiming your attention? Sometimes the simplest changes—like moving your phone to another room during dinner or setting a "no screens" rule for the first 30 minutes after waking—can create surprising ripple effects throughout your digital life.

Remember, the goal isn't digital minimalism or rejection of technology—it's intentional use that aligns with your deeper values and goals. Every small step toward more conscious technology use is a victory for your cognitive health in our increasingly connected world.

As we've explored how technology affects our attention and cognitive abilities, it's time to look behind the curtain at what's actually driving these effects. Our digital experiences don't just happen—they're carefully crafted by invisible systems designed to capture and maintain our engagement. These algorithmic engines quietly shape what we see, what we believe, and ultimately how we experience reality itself. Understanding how these algorithms work isn't just academic knowledge—it's essential for reclaiming control over your digital life and making truly informed choices about how you engage with technology.

CHAPTER 3: ALGORITHMS— PERSONALIZED EXPERIENCES AND THE ILLUSION OF CONTROL

HOW ALGORITHMS SHAPE OUR CHOICES: THE HIDDEN PUPPET MASTERS

That innocent scroll through your Instagram feed? That "quick" Amazon search? That movie recommendation you just clicked on? None of these are passive activities. Behind your screen, complex algorithms are analyzing your every click, hover, and pause—building a detailed profile of who you are and what makes you tick.

These algorithms aren't just observing; they're actively shaping your experience, guiding your choices in ways you might not even notice. And while personalization seems helpful—who doesn't want relevant content?—there's a darker reality lurking beneath the surface.

Think about it: Every time you search for running shoes, algorithms note your interest. They analyze your browsing history, past purchases, even how long you linger on certain images. They build a digital version of "you" that can sometimes predict your behavior better than your closest friends. Your e-commerce site serves up shoes you actually want, Netflix suggests shows you'll likely enjoy, and your social feeds show content matching your political leanings or interests. It feels tailor-made because it is.

This convenience comes at a cost. The personalized bubble around you slowly transforms into a "filter bubble"—an invisible wall that shields you from ideas challenging your existing beliefs. If you primarily read conservative news, algorithms will serve more conservative content. Soon, you're swimming in information that only confirms what you already believe, making contrary viewpoints seem increasingly foreign or even threatening.

I witnessed this firsthand last month when researching electric vehicles. After clicking on a few articles questioning their environmental impact, my feeds suddenly filled with content criticizing green technology. Two weeks later, a friend researching the same topic showed me her feed—packed with glowing endorsements of EVs. Same topic, completely different information universes. Have you ever compared search results with someone else and been surprised at how different they are?

The web you see is fundamentally different from the one seen by someone with different views or interests. This isn't just about politics—it affects everything from health information to consumer choices. Researching a medical condition? You might only see information supporting a specific treatment, missing potentially better alternatives. Shopping? You may never discover competing products that might better meet your needs.

More troubling is how algorithms can exploit your vulnerabilities. When advertisers analyze your online behavior, they identify your insecurities, desires, and anxieties, then target ads accordingly. What feels like your own discovery or decision often results from invisible nudges directing you toward specific choices.

The attention economy thrives on keeping you engaged, even at the cost of your mental well-being. The constant stream of curated content—designed to trigger emotional responses—fragments your attention and makes deep thinking nearly impossible. We become conditioned to consume information in bite-sized pieces, making it harder to engage with nuanced, complex ideas. The immediate gratification of the next personalized post often outweighs the value of sustained focus on something meaningful.

This algorithmic manipulation raises profound

ethical questions. Most users have no idea how their data shapes what they see, nor any real control over it. The opacity of these systems makes informed consent nearly impossible. And when algorithms inherit societal biases from their training data, they can perpetuate discrimination in employment, housing, lending, and other crucial areas.

What can we do? First, we need greater transparency from tech companies. Users deserve to understand how their information is used and what factors influence their personalized experiences. Regulations must ensure accountability and prevent exploitation, protecting privacy and addressing algorithmic bias.

As individuals, we need to become more digitally literate. Understanding how algorithms work empowers us to make conscious choices about our digital engagement and resist manipulation. This means intentionally diversifying our information sources, actively seeking viewpoints different from our own, and approaching all content with healthy skepticism. We need to regularly ask ourselves: "Why am I seeing this content? What might I be missing?"

The power of algorithms is neither inherently good nor bad—it's how they're designed and deployed that matters. By promoting transparency, accountability, and literacy, we can harness the benefits of personalization while building a more equitable and informed digital society. We must reclaim our autonomy in this algorithmically curated world, ensuring technology enhances rather than diminishes our humanity.

FILTER BUBBLES AND ECHO CHAMBERS: WHEN ALGORITHMS TRAP US

That moment when you customize your news feed seems innocent enough. You're just trying to see more of what you like and less of what you don't. But this simple act—multiplied across billions of users—has reshaped our information landscape in ways we're only beginning to understand.

Welcome to the world of filter bubbles and echo chambers, where algorithms quietly determine what information you see and, perhaps more importantly, what you don't. These invisible information cocoons might feel comfortable, but they pose serious threats to how we understand the world and relate to people different from ourselves.

Here's how it works: Every time you click, share, or linger on content, algorithms are watching. They build detailed profiles of your preferences and feed you more of what you seem to like. Soon, your digital reality becomes a mirror reflecting your existing beliefs and interests rather than a window to the wider world. Your conservative or progressive views? Reinforced. Your stance on vaccines or climate change? Validated by a stream of confirming information.

The mechanics are subtle but powerful. The algorithm notices you engage with certain viewpoints, then serves similar content, creating a feedback loop that narrows your exposure over time. What makes this especially dangerous is how invisible the process is—most people have no idea they're seeing a filtered version of reality.

I experienced this firsthand during the last election cycle. After clicking on a few articles supporting my preferred candidate, my feeds transformed into an echo chamber of like-minded content. When I finally had dinner with a friend who supported the opposing candidate, I was shocked by how differently we understood basic facts about the same events. We weren't just disagreeing on opinions—we were operating from completely different information sets. Sound familiar?

Consider someone who primarily follows conservative news sources. The algorithm, noticing this pattern, prioritizes similar content, further reinforcing that worldview. Over time, exposure to opposing perspectives becomes increasingly rare. This isn't just about politics—it affects every aspect of our information diet. Researching health topics? You might only see information confirming a particular treatment approach. Shopping decisions? You may never discover alternative products that better meet your needs.

This algorithmic cocooning has profound consequences for society. As we retreat into information silos, productive dialogue becomes nearly impossible. How can we meaningfully discuss solutions to complex problems when we can't even agree on basic facts? Echo chambers amplify polarization, making those with different views seem increasingly alien or malicious. They create environments where misinformation flourishes unchecked by contrary evidence or critical analysis.

Social media platforms exacerbate this problem. Their algorithms, designed to maximize engagement, often prioritize emotionally charged or extreme content that reinforces existing beliefs. Studies consistently show that false information spreads faster and farther than accurate information, particularly when it aligns with users' preexisting biases. Without exposure to counterarguments, conspiracy theories and misinformation can rapidly gain credibility within closed information networks.

The real-world impacts are all around us. Vaccine hesitancy, climate change denial, and political polarization all thrive in part because of these algorithmic divides. When we no longer share a common information base, the very foundation of democratic discourse crumbles.

Breaking free requires both technological solutions and personal responsibility. Platforms should redesign algorithms to prioritize diverse perspectives and reduce the amplification of potentially harmful content. They should be transparent about how content curation works, empowering users to make informed choices about their information consumption.

As individuals, we must actively cultivate media literacy and critical thinking. This means deliberately seeking out viewpoints that challenge our assumptions, engaging respectfully with those who disagree, and approaching all information— even (especially) that which confirms our beliefs— with healthy skepticism. Ask yourself: "Am I seeing a balanced picture here? What perspectives might I be missing?"

Try this experiment tomorrow: Search for a controversial topic using your regular browser, then repeat the search in an incognito window or on a public computer. The differences might surprise you—and reveal the invisible walls that have been shaping your understanding of the world.

Building a more balanced information ecosystem requires collective effort from technology companies, policymakers, educators, and individual users. The goal isn't eliminating personalization entirely— that's neither possible nor desirable—but creating systems that provide convenience without sacrificing exposure to diverse perspectives. This means designing algorithms that serve users' genuine interests, including their interest in being well-informed citizens, not just engaged consumers.

The future of informed decision-making and social cohesion depends on our ability to recognize and resist the limitations of filter bubbles. The algorithms that shape our digital lives should be tools for expanding our understanding, not narrowing it. By mindfully engaging with diverse sources and demanding more transparent, responsible algorithmic design, we can begin to bridge the divides that threaten our collective ability to address the pressing challenges of our time.

THE ILLUSION OF CONTROL: UNDERSTANDING ALGORITHMIC MANIPULATION

The seemingly effortless personalization offered by today's digital platforms masks a complex interplay between algorithmic design and human psychology. While we experience the convenience of tailored recommendations and seemingly customized content, a deeper examination reveals a subtle yet powerful manipulation: the illusion of control.

As humans, we crave agency—the feeling that we're directing our own lives through autonomous decisions. Algorithms cleverly exploit this desire by providing a carefully curated selection of options that appear to cater to our individual preferences. The result? A sense of personalization that reinforces our belief in our own agency, even when the range of choices has been subtly constrained.

Consider your last online shopping experience. Did it feel like you were freely browsing through products, making independent discoveries? In reality, recommendation engines were analyzing your browsing history, purchase patterns, and even social media activity to predict what might appeal to you. The product suggestions you received were tailored to your perceived interests, subtly guiding your purchasing journey. You felt like you were choosing, but your options were already pre-shaped by the algorithm's predictions.

I noticed this recently while planning a vacation. After searching for "beach destinations," suddenly my entire digital world became saturated with coastal getaways. Hotels in mountain regions or cultural cities—options I might have enjoyed just as much—simply disappeared from view. My seemingly "free" choice had been quietly narrowed to fit what the algorithm determined I wanted. Have you ever noticed how quickly your online world shifts after showing interest in something new?

This manipulation extends beyond shopping. The design of choice architecture—how options are presented to you—significantly influences your decisions. When streaming platforms highlight certain shows in prominent positions or display "recommended for you" selections first, they're not just helping you find content—they're strategically guiding your viewing habits toward specific choices. The options buried four screens deep might be better matches for your actual tastes, but their placement makes them practically invisible.

The power of defaults further strengthens this illusion. Most people never change the default settings on their devices or platforms, accepting pre-selected options without realizing how these defaults shape their experience. Your social media privacy settings, news feed algorithms, and search engine parameters are initially configured to maximize data collection and engagement—not necessarily to serve your best interests. Yet these defaults feel like neutral starting points rather than deliberate design choices.

Our cognitive biases make us particularly vulnerable to these manipulations. Confirmation bias—our tendency to favor information that confirms existing beliefs—works perfectly with algorithms designed to show us more of what we already like. This creates a comfortable but limiting cycle where we increasingly see content that reinforces our worldview while contradictory information gradually disappears from our feeds.

The availability heuristic compounds this effect. We tend to judge the importance or frequency of something based on how easily examples come to mind. When algorithms repeatedly expose us to certain types of content—whether political perspectives, product categories, or lifestyle choices —these become more mentally available, creating a distorted perception of reality. After my recent search for running shoes, it suddenly seemed like everyone was talking about fitness and athletic gear— not because the world had changed, but because my algorithmic lens had narrowed.

This algorithmic shaping extends to our identities and social connections. The friends, groups, and content suggested to us on social platforms influence how we see ourselves and others. The algorithm's predictions about who we might want to connect with can reinforce existing social bubbles or steer us toward particular communities, affecting our sense of belonging and social identity.

The consequences of these manipulations aren't trivial. When we believe we're making free choices while actually being guided by invisible algorithms, we surrender important aspects of our autonomy. Our worldviews narrow, our consumption patterns become more predictable, and our agency diminishes —all while maintaining the comforting illusion that we're in control.

What's particularly insidious is how seamless and invisible this manipulation has become. Unlike traditional advertising, which we recognize as persuasion, algorithmic influence operates below our awareness. It feels natural, personalized, and helpful rather than manipulative or limiting.

So how do we reclaim genuine agency in this environment? The first step is awareness—recognizing the invisible forces shaping our online experiences. When recommendations appear, ask yourself: "Why am I seeing this? What data might have triggered this suggestion? What might I not be seeing as a result?"

Next, actively diversify your inputs. Seek out information sources and perspectives that challenge your existing views. Use different search engines, browse in private mode occasionally, or deliberately explore topics outside your usual interests. These practices won't eliminate algorithmic influence, but they can help expand the range of content you encounter.

Consider adjusting your privacy settings and permissions on various platforms. Limiting data collection can reduce the precision of personalization while protecting your privacy. Similarly, periodically clearing your browsing history and cookies can help reset some algorithmic predictions, providing a slightly fresher slate.

Most importantly, practice mindful consumption. Before clicking, sharing, or purchasing, pause and consider whether you're making a genuinely independent choice or being nudged by sophisticated algorithms. This momentary reflection can help restore a measure of agency in your digital interactions.

The goal isn't to eliminate personalization—which does offer genuine benefits—but to engage with it more consciously. By understanding the psychological mechanisms behind algorithmic manipulation, we can navigate the digital world with greater awareness, making choices that truly reflect our interests and values rather than merely reinforcing patterns identified by algorithms.

What small step will you take today to peek behind the curtain of your personalized digital experience? The journey toward digital autonomy begins with this kind of curiosity and intentional engagement with the technologies that increasingly shape our lives.

ALGORITHMIC TRANSPARENCY AND ACCOUNTABILITY: THE NEED FOR ETHICAL FRAMEWORKS

The illusion of control created by algorithms extends far beyond consumer choices. It permeates various aspects of our lives, from the news we read to the opportunities we're offered, raising critical questions about transparency, accountability, and fairness in our increasingly automated world.

Imagine applying for a loan and being rejected without explanation. Or picture yourself being passed over for a job interview because an algorithm screened out your application based on criteria you'll never know. These scenarios happen daily, affecting life-changing opportunities with little recourse for those impacted. The opacity of algorithmic decision-making creates a fundamental power imbalance between those who design and deploy these systems and those subject to their determinations.

Many of today's most influential algorithms function as "black boxes"—their internal workings hidden from view, inscrutable even to their creators. This lack of transparency makes it nearly impossible to identify and correct biases, assess potential risks, or hold anyone accountable when things go wrong. It's like being judged by a hidden tribunal that never explains its reasoning.

I witnessed this firsthand when my friend Maria— a highly qualified nurse with years of experience— kept getting rejected from hospital positions after moving to a new city. Application after application disappeared into the void with only automated rejections in response. Only months later did she discover the likely culprit: an automated screening system flagging her eight-month employment gap (for cancer treatment) as a "job-hopping risk."

The system never disclosed this criteria, and human recruiters never reviewed her impressive qualifications. How many qualified candidates have you known who were similarly filtered out by invisible parameters?

The challenge of accountability becomes even more complex when considering how responsibility diffuses across multiple parties. When an algorithmic system makes a harmful or discriminatory decision, who bears responsibility? The developer who created the algorithm? The company that deployed it? The data scientists who trained it? Or perhaps the individuals who provided the training data that contained embedded biases? This diffusion of responsibility creates a situation where no one person or entity is clearly answerable for algorithmic harms.

The rapid pace of technological advancement only exacerbates these issues. New algorithms and applications emerge constantly, often before ethical considerations have been adequately addressed. Regulatory frameworks struggle to keep pace, creating a vacuum where powerful technologies operate with minimal oversight. Meanwhile, the potential for harm—discriminatory lending practices, biased hiring systems, manipulative recommendation engines—continues to grow.

Addressing these challenges requires a multi-faceted approach. First, we need greater algorithmic transparency. This doesn't necessarily mean publishing proprietary code or complex mathematical formulas. Rather, it involves providing clear, accessible explanations of how algorithmic systems make decisions, what factors they consider, and how these factors are weighted. Users should understand what data is being collected about them and how it influences the content or opportunities they're shown.

Have you ever wondered why you see specific content in your social media feed? Platforms could provide simple explanations: "You're seeing this post because you recently engaged with similar content" or "This advertisement appears based on your location and browsing history." This type of transparency gives users insight into the factors shaping their experiences and the ability to make more informed choices about their digital engagement.

Beyond transparency, we need robust accountability mechanisms. This includes regular algorithmic audits by independent third parties to assess fairness, accuracy, and potential biases. It means creating clear channels for users to appeal algorithmic decisions that affect them and processes for addressing valid concerns. And it requires establishing legal frameworks that assign responsibility when algorithmic systems cause harm, ensuring affected individuals have recourse.

The development of ethical frameworks for algorithm design and deployment is equally crucial. These frameworks should prioritize fundamental values like fairness, non-discrimination, privacy, and human autonomy. They should guide developers in considering the potential societal impacts of their work and making design choices that mitigate harms. And they should establish clear red lines—applications or approaches that are simply too risky or potentially harmful to deploy, regardless of their technical feasibility.

Participatory approaches to algorithm development can also help. By involving diverse stakeholders —including potential users and those who might be affected by algorithmic decisions—in the design process, developers can better anticipate potential issues and ensure systems meet the needs of varied populations. This collaborative approach helps bridge the gap between technical possibilities and human realities, resulting in more responsible and effective technological solutions.

Education plays a vital role too. As citizens in an algorithmic age, we all need a basic understanding of how these systems work, their limitations, and how to critically evaluate their outputs. Schools should incorporate digital literacy into their curricula, teaching students not just how to use technology but how to think critically about its influence on their lives and society. Adults need accessible resources to develop similar skills, empowering them to navigate an increasingly algorithmic world with confidence and discernment.

Finally, organizational culture matters enormously. Companies that develop and deploy algorithms should foster a culture of responsibility, encouraging employees to consider the ethical implications of their work and providing channels for raising concerns. This includes diverse hiring practices to ensure varied perspectives inform technology development and rewarding careful consideration of social impact alongside technical innovation.

The path toward greater algorithmic transparency and accountability isn't straightforward, but it's essential for creating a technological future that respects human dignity and autonomy. By demanding greater openness from technology companies, supporting thoughtful regulation, and developing our own digital literacy, we can help shape a world where algorithms serve human flourishing rather than undermining it.

What questions should you be asking about the algorithms influencing your daily life? Start with simple inquiries: Why am I seeing this content? What data is being collected about me? How can I appeal decisions that affect me? These basic questions begin the important work of bringing algorithmic systems into the light, where they can be examined, improved, and held accountable for their impacts on our lives and society.

NAVIGATING THE ALGORITHMIC

LANDSCAPE: STRATEGIES FOR CRITICAL CONSUMPTION

We've uncovered the powerful influence algorithms have on our lives, shaping everything from shopping choices to political beliefs. But understanding the problem is only half the battle. The real challenge? Developing practical strategies to navigate this invisible landscape with intention and awareness.

Think of yourself as an explorer in unfamiliar territory. You need tools, knowledge, and a healthy dose of skepticism to find your way. Here's your survival guide for the algorithmic wilderness.

RECOGNIZE THE INVISIBLE GUIDES

First, accept that algorithms aren't neutral observers —they're active participants in your decision-making process. That product recommendation? That news article that seems tailor-made for your interests? They didn't appear by accident.

Start by questioning what you see online. When your social media feed shows you a political story that perfectly aligns with your views, ask yourself:

Who created this content?

Why am I seeing it now?

What might be missing from this perspective?

How might someone with different beliefs view this?

Remember, algorithms are designed to show you what you'll engage with—not necessarily what's true, balanced, or helpful for your growth.

BREAK OUT OF YOUR BUBBLE

The most dangerous aspect of algorithmic filtering isn't what it shows you—it's what it hides. The solution? Deliberately seek diversity in your information diet.

Try these practical steps:

Follow people who challenge your thinking

Use different search engines for important research

Read news from outlets across the political spectrum

Join online communities with diverse membership

When I started following people with opposing political views, I initially felt uncomfortable. Their perspectives seemed wrong, even offensive sometimes. Over time, I gained valuable insights into how different people think about the same issues.

I didn't always change my mind, but I developed a more nuanced understanding of complex topics.

EVALUATE SOURCES LIKE A DETECTIVE

In a world where anyone can publish content, critical evaluation skills are your best defense. Before accepting information as fact, investigate:

Credibility: Does the source have expertise? A track record of accuracy?

Evidence: Are claims backed by verifiable data? Or just anecdotes?

Transparency: Does the source acknowledge limitations? Disclose conflicts?

Motivation: What does the publisher gain from your engagement?

When you encounter a health claim or political statistic that seems shocking, take a moment before sharing. Check if reputable sources confirm the information. Look for primary sources of data rather than relying on someone else's interpretation.

Last week, I almost shared an alarming article about a new health risk until I noticed the site was selling "protective" supplements at the bottom of the page. A quick check revealed no mainstream medical sources supported their claims.

Have you ever caught yourself about to share something before verifying its accuracy?

GUARD YOUR ATTENTION DELIBERATELY

Your attention is valuable currency in the digital economy—treat it that way. Instead of mindlessly consuming whatever algorithms serve up, make conscious choices about how you spend your limited cognitive resources.

Try these practical approaches:

Set time limits for social media use

Disable non-essential notifications

Curate your feeds to prioritize quality over quantity

Schedule regular "deep work" sessions without digital interruptions

I used to reflexively reach for my phone during any moment of boredom or discomfort.

Now I've trained myself to pause and ask, "Is this really how I want to use the next 15 minutes of my life?" Often, the answer is no—and I choose something more meaningful instead.

JOIN FORCES WITH OTHERS

Individual efforts matter, but collective action creates real change. Support organizations advocating for:

Greater algorithmic transparency

Stronger data privacy protections

Independent audits of powerful algorithms

Media literacy education in schools

Talk with friends and family about these issues. Share what you've learned about algorithmic influence. The more people understand how these systems work, the more power we collectively have to demand better.

RECLAIM YOUR AGENCY

Remember that you are more than the sum of your clicks and views. Algorithms may suggest what you might like, but only you can decide what you truly value.

The goal isn't to abandon technology—it's to use it intentionally. Think of algorithms as tools rather than authorities. They can make recommendations, but you make the final decisions about what to read, believe, buy, and share.

When you notice yourself being pulled into a rabbit hole of content, pause and ask: "Is this serving me? Is this helping me become the person I want to be?" If not, redirect your attention elsewhere.

Navigating the algorithmic landscape takes effort, but the reward is genuine autonomy in a world designed to influence you at every turn. By developing these critical skills, you're not just protecting yourself from manipulation—you're contributing to a healthier information ecosystem for everyone.

The journey toward digital literacy is ongoing. The algorithms evolve, and so must our strategies. But with awareness, intention, and practice, you can transform from a passive consumer into an active, discerning participant in our shared digital world.

What small step will you take today to reclaim some control over your algorithmic experience? Perhaps it's following someone with different views, setting a timer for your social media use, or simply pausing to question why you're seeing particular content. Each mindful action chips away at the invisible walls that limit your digital horizon.

While algorithms powerfully shape what we see online, there's another dimension to our digital lives that's equally transformative: how we present ourselves in these spaces. The content delivered to us is only half the equation—what we choose to share and how we construct our online personas forms the other half of this complex relationship. Just as algorithms curate our incoming information, we carefully curate the outgoing signals that form our digital identities. Let's examine this fascinating dance of self-presentation and explore how our online selves both reflect and reshape who we truly are.

CHAPTER 4: CONSTRUCTING ONLINE IDENTITIES: THE ART OF DIGITAL SELF-PRESENTATION

Think about the last photo you posted online. Did you snap it once and immediately share it? Or—be honest here—did you take multiple shots, choose the best one, add a filter, craft the perfect caption, and strategically time your post for maximum engagement?

Don't worry, you're not alone. We're all playing this fascinating game online, crafting versions of ourselves that exist somewhere between who we really are and who we aspire to be. The digital world has given us an unprecedented canvas for identity exploration, allowing you to shape how others perceive you with a freedom that face-to-face interactions rarely permit.

WHY WE CRAFT OUR DIGITAL SELVES

For some of us, online spaces provide a rare freedom. Remember that painfully shy kid in high school who barely spoke a word? I once worked with a young man like this who transformed into a confident, witty presence on Discord—finding his voice in a space where he could thoughtfully compose his thoughts before sharing them. Or consider the corporate accountant who keeps her creative passions hidden at work but builds a vibrant Instagram community around her pottery hobby. Have you ever had a side of yourself that only feels safe to express online?

The internet creates breathing room between your actions and immediate social judgment, allowing for authentic exploration that might feel too risky in person.

For others, the driving force is connection and belonging. You craft profiles that signal your tribe affiliations—whether through the music you share, the causes you support, or the aesthetic you cultivate. Think about how the parent struggling with a child's rare medical condition finds life-changing support in specialized Facebook groups, or how a young professional moving to a new city discovers community through local Reddit threads. We shape our online personas to find our people, often experiencing powerful validation when we succeed.

The complexity arises when that desire for acceptance leads to calculated impression management. Let's face it—we've all become amateur publicists, carefully curating our digital presence to highlight our best moments while strategically concealing our struggles. You post the vacation photos but not the credit card bill that followed. You share the job promotion but not the burnout you're feeling. You show the perfectly plated homemade meal but not the kitchen disaster that preceded it. Sound familiar?

THE MANY FACES WE WEAR ONLINE

The strategies you employ likely vary depending on the platform and context. Some of us present highly polished, aspirational versions of ourselves— the highlight reel of our lives designed to impress or influence. You showcase achievements, carefully composed photos, and evidence of your most interesting moments.

Others create personas distinctly separate from their offline selves—perhaps a gamer tag identity with different personality traits, a pseudonymous Twitter account for political opinions, or an artistic alter-ego for creative expression. These separate digital identities can provide liberating playgrounds for exploring different aspects of yourself.

Some strive for authenticity—sharing both successes and struggles in a deliberate attempt to connect more genuinely. Yet even "authentic" sharing involves curation—decisions about which vulnerabilities feel safe to expose and which remain private. Have you noticed how even the most "real" influencers still carefully manage which unfiltered moments they choose to share?

The platforms themselves shape these choices through their design. Instagram's visual emphasis pushes you toward aesthetic perfection. LinkedIn rewards professional accomplishments. TikTok values entertaining, quick-witted content. Each platform subtly trains you in its native language of engagement, guiding how you present yourself in that particular digital space.

WHEN YOUR DIGITAL AND PHYSICAL WORLDS COLLIDE

What's fascinating is how these online identities increasingly bleed into your offline life. The boundaries between your digital and physical selves grow more permeable every day.

A tough day at the office might prompt a venting session on Twitter, which then shapes how colleagues perceive you the next morning. The confidence gained from positive feedback on your YouTube channel might empower you to speak up more in physical meetings. The supportive community you've built around your mental health journey online might give you courage to be more open with friends and family offline.

These aren't separate lives anymore—they're interconnected facets of your whole self, each influencing the other in ongoing feedback loops.

THE PSYCHOLOGICAL WEIGHT OF MANAGING YOUR DIGITAL SELF

Managing online identities comes with significant psychological costs. The pressure to maintain curated personas can be exhausting—like having a part-time job as your own PR manager. I've worked with clients who spend hours each day managing their online presence, constantly anxious about maintaining the perfect image they've created.

The constant exposure to others' highlight reels triggers painful social comparison, making your normal, messy life seem inadequate by contrast. The gap between your online presentation and your reality can create cognitive dissonance. Are you being authentic or performing? Where does the "real you" end and the curated version begin?

Then there's the vulnerability of putting yourself out there—the risk of criticism, rejection, or outright cruelty from strangers hiding behind keyboards. A negative comment on a post you spent hours crafting can sting for days, making you second-guess everything about yourself.

Yet online identity construction also offers profound benefits. Finding communities of like-minded people can provide life-changing support for those who feel isolated in their physical surroundings. The freedom to emphasize different aspects of your personality can facilitate self-discovery and growth. Positive feedback can build confidence that translates to other areas of life.

FINDING BALANCE IN A DIGITAL WORLD

Understanding why you construct online identities and how they affect you is crucial for navigating the digital landscape mindfully. Rather than passively falling into patterns driven by platforms designed to maximize engagement, you can make intentional choices about how you present yourself and interact online.

Consider periodically asking yourself:

Who am I trying to impress, and why does their approval matter to me?

What parts of myself am I hiding, and what would happen if I shared them?

Does my online presence reflect my actual values or just

what gets the most validation?

How do I feel after spending time on different platforms —energized or depleted?

The goal isn't to abandon self-presentation—that's part of human social nature, online or off—but to engage with it consciously. Sometimes a carefully curated post makes perfect sense; other times, authentic vulnerability might serve you better.

In the end, your online identities are neither wholly false nor completely authentic, but complex expressions of who you are, who you aspire to be, and how you wish to be seen. By understanding the psychology behind these digital personas, you can use them as tools for connection and self-expression rather than becoming trapped in exhausting performances or harmful comparisons.

Your digital self is here to stay. The question is whether you'll let it control you, or whether you'll mindfully shape it to enrich rather than diminish your lived experience.

The construction of our digital identities doesn't happen in isolation—it occurs within the context of our relationships with others. As we craft these online personas, we're simultaneously transforming how we connect, communicate, and build intimacy with the people in our lives. The same technologies that allow us to present carefully curated versions of ourselves are fundamentally reshaping our most precious connections—with romantic partners, family members, friends, and even casual acquaintances. The next frontier in understanding technology's impact on our lives is examining how these digital tools are transforming the very nature of human connection itself.

CHAPTER 5: TECHNOLOGY AND RELATIONSHIPS: FINDING BALANCE IN A CONNECTED WORLD

LOVE IN THE TIME OF SMARTPHONES: HOW TECHNOLOGY RESHAPES OUR CONNECTIONS

God, I hate that moment.

You know the one.

You're mid-sentence, explaining something important about your day, when your dinner companion's eyes flick down to the soft blue glow beneath the table.

Their "uh-huh" becomes a bit too automatic. You falter, wondering if you should just stop talking until they look up again.

It's not like we planned this strange new world of half-present conversations. Somehow we stumbled into it, one small choice at a time, until suddenly we're all doing this awkward dance around our devices.

Remember when having dinner meant actually looking at each other? When a pinging notification wouldn't interrupt every significant moment? These days, I find myself pathetically grateful when someone puts their phone face-down on the table – a small gesture that says, "You matter more than whatever might pop up on this screen." The bar has sunk that low.

Yet here's the confounding part: technology has also given us remarkable ways to stay connected across time and distance. Those late-night texts when someone's struggling and needs support without judgment. Video calls that let families separated by oceans maintain meaningful relationships. These aren't small gifts in our increasingly dispersed world.

So we live in this maddening contradiction. Our relationships are simultaneously broader and shallower, more constant and more interrupted, more convenient and more complicated than ever before in human history.

Throughout this chapter, I won't pretend there are easy answers to this mess we've created. You won't find some magical three-step plan to fix your technology-addled relationships. What you will find is an honest exploration of how our devices have reshaped everything from how we fall in love to how we raise our kids, along with some hard-earned wisdom about creating connections that technology enhances rather than erodes.

DIGITAL DATING: FINDING LOVE THROUGH ALGORITHMS

I've observed three distinct reactions to dating apps among people. First, the evangelists who credit these platforms with connecting them to partners they never would have met otherwise—different social circles, neighborhoods, or routines that would have kept them ships passing in the night. Then there are the casualties who describe months of swiping, dozens of disappointing first dates, and a growing cynicism about the whole enterprise. And finally, the burnt-out users who lament the monotony: "It's just the same conversations over and over. 'How's your Tuesday?' 'What neighborhood are you in?' Kill me now."

The truth? All these perspectives have merit.

Dating apps have utterly transformed romantic relationships, for better and worse. Since Match.com pioneered digital dating in the 90s, we've developed a dizzying ecosystem of options. Christian? JDate not your scene? Vegetarian who loves hiking? Dog owner seeking same? There's an app perfectly calibrated to your preferences, slicing the dating pool into ever-more-specific puddles.

The upside is obvious: your potential matches have exploded beyond whoever happens to be at the same bar on Friday night. For people in small towns, with unconventional schedules, or with specific requirements in a partner, these apps are genuinely liberating. Single parents with demanding schedules can browse potential matches during those rare quiet moments instead of trying to arrange babysitters for hit-or-miss nights out.

But the poisoned apple of dating apps is what psychologists call "choice overload." Every disappointing date gets measured against the infinite possibilities waiting on your phone. Every minor flaw becomes magnified when perfection seems just a swipe away. People become disposable in a way that feels almost inhuman.

The evolution of courtship rituals has been fascinatingly weird, too. The old dance had clear steps: meet someone, flirt cautiously, exchange numbers, call after the mandatory three-day waiting period (remember that madness?), plan a proper date for the weekend.

Now? You match on Tuesday, start messaging immediately, dive down the rabbit hole of their Instagram from 2016, discover you both love Thai food and have strong opinions about Game of Thrones, share deeply personal stories about your childhood trauma by Thursday, and schedule drinks for Friday—all before laying eyes on each other in real life. It's backwards. We build emotional intimacy before establishing the most basic physical comfort level. No wonder first dates have gotten so awkward.

Beyond this bizarro intimacy timeline, we face the inescapable fact that profiles are curated fictions. Even when not deliberately deceptive, they're carefully constructed highlight reels. You rarely see a bio that admits to talking too much when nervous, having a terrible sense of direction, or strong opinions about condiments that might become annoying over time.

Instead, we get carefully angled selfies, the one photo from that charity 5K, and bios crafted to seem simultaneously sophisticated yet approachable, ambitious yet chill, unique yet non-threatening. It's exhausting for everyone.

If you're trying to navigate this mess (and let's face it, most single people are), here's what actually works:

1. **Meet in person quickly.** Not in a creepy, unsafe way. But after establishing basic non-serial-killer vibes, get to an actual face-to-face. Nothing kills potential faster than weeks of perfect texting chemistry followed by a real-life meetup that feels like conversing with a mannequin.

2. **Use recent, accurate photos.** Yes, you looked amazing at your cousin's wedding three

years and twenty pounds ago. But surprising someone with your current appearance isn't the rom-com meet-cute you think it is—it's a breach of trust before you've even ordered drinks.

3. **Decide what you want before you swipe.** The "I'm just seeing what's out there" approach works about as well for dating apps as it does for late-night grocery shopping when starving. You'll end up with a cart full of regrets.

4. **Take mental health breaks.** Dating apps are literally designed by the same psychological principles as slot machines. The variable reward system is brutally effective at keeping you hooked, even when it's making you miserable. When you start feeling like human connection is a game you're losing, delete the app for a month.

5. **Don't take rejection personally.** This is brutally hard advice to follow, but essential. Someone rejecting your carefully curated profile says nothing about your worth as a human being. They don't know you. They're making split-second decisions based on arbitrary preferences and whatever mood

they're in while sitting on the toilet swiping through faces.

The most resilient digital daters see apps as just one channel for meeting people, not their entire strategy. They still say yes to setups from friends, strike up conversations at events, and participate in activities they genuinely enjoy. Because ultimately, the apps can only introduce you to someone—they can't create the messy, wonderful, complicated bond of two humans choosing each other day after day.

KEEPING THE SPARK ALIVE: TECHNOLOGY IN LONG-TERM RELATIONSHIPS

Many long-term couples eventually find themselves in a routine where technology becomes more of a barrier than a bridge. After the initial excitement fades, many couples find themselves in the same house but different digital worlds—one partner browsing social media while the other streams videos, together physically but mentally elsewhere.

The impact of technology on established relationships differs from its effect on new ones.

In long-term partnerships, the challenge isn't discovering each other—it's staying present and engaged after the novelty fades. Digital devices can become easy escapes from the sometimes challenging work of maintaining intimacy.

Have you noticed how much easier it is to scroll through social media than to have a difficult conversation with your partner? Or how often you reach for your phone when bored or uncomfortable? This isn't coincidental—these devices are designed to capture your attention, offering constant novelty that can make the familiar person beside you seem less interesting by comparison.

The impacts are measurable. Studies show that the mere presence of a phone—even face-down on a table—reduces the quality of conversation between partners and decreases reported feelings of closeness and trust. This phenomenon, dubbed "phubbing" (phone snubbing), has been linked to decreased relationship satisfaction and increased conflict.

But technology isn't inherently harmful to relationships. In fact, when used mindfully, it can significantly enhance connection between partners. Consider how different tools can serve different relationship needs:

Texting can maintain connection throughout the day between busy partners. Quick messages saying "Thinking of you" or "Good luck with your presentation today" create touchpoints that keep you emotionally tethered when physically apart.

Video calls enable deeper connection for couples navigating distance. Being able to see facial expressions and hear voice tones provides much richer communication than text alone.

Shared digital calendars reduce logistical friction, allowing you to coordinate schedules without constant back-and-forth.

Relationship apps designed specifically for couples can facilitate everything from organizing date nights to guiding meaningful conversations to maintaining intimate connection.

The key difference between technology that enhances versus undermines relationships lies in intention. Are you using digital tools to deepen your connection, or to avoid it?

Many couples have found success establishing new technology boundaries. Creating tech-free zones (bedroom and dining room) and tech-free times (dinner and the first hour after both getting home) can make a significant difference. Using text messages throughout the day not just for logistics but to flirt and express appreciation helps maintain connection. Implementing a weekly "digital sunset"—one evening where all devices are turned off completely—can create space for deeper connection.

Here are practical strategies any couple can

implement:

1. **Establish tech-free zones and times.** Designate specific areas in your home and periods in your day that remain device-free. The bedroom is especially important—phones in the bedroom interfere with both intimacy and sleep quality.

2. **Create intentional transition rituals.** The shift from work to home is important. Try implementing a 15-minute no-phone policy when you first reunite with your partner to properly reconnect before devices come back out.

3. **Use technology to enhance, not replace.** Instead of mindlessly scrolling while together, use technology for shared experiences—cook together using a new recipe app, take an online dance class in your living room, or use a stargazing app during an evening walk.

4. **Schedule regular digital detoxes.** Whether it's a device-free dinner once a week or a full weekend away from screens every few months, creating intentional breaks from technology allows space for reconnection.

5. **Notice your escape patterns.** Pay attention to when you reach for your phone during interactions with your partner. Is it when conversations get difficult? When you're bored? These patterns reveal important information about your relationship dynamics.

Remember that technology itself isn't the problem—it's how we use it. Your smartphone can either be a wall between you and your partner or a bridge connecting you throughout the day. The difference lies in your awareness and intention.

DIGITAL PARENTING: RAISING CHILDREN IN A CONNECTED WORLD

Parents today face challenges that no previous generation has navigated: raising children in a world where digital devices are ubiquitous and social interactions increasingly happen online. Adolescents may spend hours alone with their devices, maintaining complex social lives that are largely invisible to parents. The digital drama of comments, likes, and group chats can consume a teenager's emotional energy while appearing to parents as just "screen time."

This creates one of the most profound challenges facing modern parents: raising children in a digital landscape that bears little resemblance to our own childhoods. The devices and platforms that connect kids to their peers also expose them to unprecedented pressures, influences, and risks.

If you're a parent, you've likely wondered: How much screen time is too much?

At what age should my child get a smartphone?

How do I protect them online without invading their privacy?

These questions have no simple answers, but understanding the impact of technology on child development can help you navigate these complex waters.

Unlike adults, who witnessed the gradual digital transformation of society, today's children are true digital natives—they've never known a world without smartphones, social media, and instant access to information. This shapes their development in fundamental ways:

Socially, children now maintain friendships through a complex mix of in-person and online interactions. Social status is determined not just by schoolyard popularity but by social media metrics—likes, followers, comments. For many teens, their online presence has become inseparable from their identity.

Cognitively, growing up with constant access to information creates different learning patterns.

Today's kids may have weaker memorization skills but stronger abilities to find and synthesize information from multiple sources. Their attention spans are adapted to switching between different inputs rather than sustaining focus on a single task.

Emotionally, children face unique challenges. Social media creates new avenues for comparison, exclusion, and bullying. The carefully curated highlight reels they see online can trigger feelings of inadequacy. And the dopamine-driven feedback loops of games and social platforms can establish patterns that resemble addiction.

Parenting effectively in this environment requires a balanced approach—neither fearfully restricting all technology use nor allowing unlimited, unsupervised access. Here are strategies that successful digital parents employ:

1. **Focus on teaching judgment rather than imposing control.** While monitoring and limits are necessary, especially for younger children, your ultimate goal should be raising kids who can make wise decisions about technology use. This means gradually increasing freedom as they demonstrate responsibility.

2. **Create a family media plan.** Rather than ad-hoc rules that change with your mood, establish clear guidelines about when and

where devices can be used, what platforms are allowed at what ages, and consequences for breaking these agreements. Revisit and revise this plan as children mature.

3. **Model healthy technology habits.** Children learn more from what you do than what you say. If you're constantly checking your phone while telling them to limit screen time, your message loses credibility. Demonstrate the balanced relationship with technology that you want them to develop.

4. **Make digital literacy a family priority.** Teach critical thinking skills about online content. Help children understand how algorithms work, why certain content appears in their feeds, and how to evaluate the credibility of information. Discuss concepts like digital footprints and the permanence of online actions.

5. **Keep communication open.** Create regular opportunities to discuss what's happening in their digital lives without judgment. Ask about the apps they use, the people they interact with online, and the content they enjoy. Stay curious rather than critical.

6. **Prioritize privacy and safety.** Teach children about protecting personal information, the concept of consent regarding photos and information sharing, and strategies for handling inappropriate contact. Make sure they know they can come to you if something uncomfortable happens online.

7. **Balance online and offline experiences.** Ensure that digital activities complement rather than replace in-person social interaction, physical activity, creative expression, and other developmental experiences.

Research shows that a measured approach works better than either extreme restriction or complete permissiveness. When children discover concerning content or experience online problems, they need to feel comfortable discussing these issues with their parents rather than hiding them for fear of punishment or device confiscation.

Every child and family is different, and the right approach for your family will depend on your values, your child's temperament, and your specific circumstances. The most important thing is staying engaged with your child's digital life—not through surveillance but through genuine interest and ongoing conversation.

Remember that you're not just managing their current technology use; you're teaching them skills they'll need for a lifetime in an increasingly digital world. By approaching digital parenting with thoughtfulness and flexibility, you can help your children develop a healthy relationship with technology that enhances rather than diminishes their lives.

FRIENDSHIP IN THE FACEBOOK AGE: MAINTAINING AUTHENTIC CONNECTIONS

Social media has transformed our concept of friendship—expanding our networks while potentially diluting the meaning of connection. A typical social media user might have hundreds or even thousands of "friends" online, but research consistently shows that meaningful social circles remain much smaller.

Think about your own social circles. You might have hundreds or even thousands of "friends" online, but how many of those people do you truly know? How many would you call during a crisis or celebrate with during life's big moments?

The evolution of friendship in the digital age presents a fascinating paradox. Technology gives us unprecedented tools to maintain connections across time and distance. People regularly chat with friends who live on different continents, sharing photos, updates, and maintaining relationships that would have faded in previous generations. Yet simultaneously, studies show increasing rates of loneliness and social isolation, suggesting that our expanding digital networks aren't satisfying our deep human need for genuine connection.

The distinction lies in quality versus quantity. Digital platforms excel at helping us maintain weak ties—those acquaintances and casual connections that form our extended social network. These relationships have value; they expand our access to different perspectives, opportunities, and information. However, they cannot replace the close, intimate friendships that research consistently links to happiness and wellbeing.

Strong friendships require several elements that digital communication makes easier to overlook:

Vulnerability is essential for deep connection, yet online interactions often favor curated perfection over authentic sharing. When was the last time you posted about your genuine struggles rather than your achievements?

Presence involves giving someone your full attention —something increasingly rare in an age of constant notifications and divided focus. A friend sitting across from you while repeatedly checking their phone isn't truly present, regardless of physical proximity.

Reciprocity in friendship means equal investment in

the relationship. Digital communication can create imbalances where interactions become performative rather than reciprocal—think of the person who posts constant updates but never engages with others' content.

Shared experiences form the foundation of many close friendships. While virtual experiences can be meaningful, they typically don't create the same depth of connection as facing challenges or celebrating milestones together in person.

So how do you maintain authentic friendships in this complex landscape? Consider these approaches:

1. **Distinguish between your social circles.** Anthropologist Robin Dunbar suggests humans can maintain about 150 meaningful social connections, with only 3-5 truly intimate relationships. Be intentional about which relationships you're actively nurturing versus passively maintaining.

2. **Deepen digital communication.** Not all online interaction is superficial. A thoughtful email, a private message sharing a vulnerable truth, or a video call allowing face-to-face conversation can nurture meaningful connection. The medium matters less than the content and intention.

3. **Create boundaries around friendship time.** When you're with friends, consider implementing a "phones away" policy to ensure genuine presence. The friend who's half engaged with you and half scrolling isn't experiencing the full benefit of your time together—and neither are you.

4. **Use technology to facilitate in-person connection.** Apps for finding events, coordinating gatherings, or discovering shared interests can help translate online connections into real-world friendships. Technology works best as a bridge to in-person interaction, not a replacement for it.

5. **Practice digital discernment.** Before sharing personal news broadly on social platforms, consider: Who really needs to know this? Might certain friends deserve a more personal form of communication? Sometimes a direct message or phone call to your closest friends before posting publicly acknowledges the special place they hold in your life.

Many people report that online interactions, while convenient, often don't provide the same depth of emotional satisfaction as in-person meetings.

The absence of nonverbal cues and physical presence can limit the fulfillment we derive from digital connections, even when they help maintain relationships across distances.

This doesn't mean abandoning social media—these platforms offer valuable ways to maintain broader social connections that enrich our lives. Rather, it's about being intentional about how you use different communication channels with different people in your life.

Consider creating a friendship communication hierarchy. For your innermost circle, prioritize one-on-one, high-quality interactions—calls, personal messages, or in-person meetings. For your broader social network, group messages and social media provide efficient ways to stay connected without depleting your limited social energy.

Remember that real friendship has always required effort and attention. Technology simply offers new tools—neither inherently better nor worse than previous methods of connection. The key is using these tools mindfully, recognizing when they enhance genuine connection and when they create an illusion of closeness without the substance.

By approaching your digital social life with intention rather than simply following the paths of least resistance, you can cultivate a rich social landscape that includes both broad networks and deep, nourishing friendships.

FAMILY TIES: NAVIGATING TECHNOLOGY ACROSS GENERATIONS

Family relationships present unique technological challenges compared to friendships or romantic partnerships. Families span generations, each with different comfort levels, skills, and preferences regarding technology. They involve complex power dynamics that shift over time—parents who once controlled their children's technology use later rely on those same children to navigate new digital tools. And family obligations often create expectations about communication that don't exist in voluntary relationships.

Have you noticed how different generations in your family approach technology? Perhaps you have teenage children who seem physically attached to their devices while your parents struggle to attach a photo to an email. Or maybe you're the parent trying to understand why your child needs to maintain Snapchat streaks with friends they see every day at school. These differences reflect not just technical skills but fundamentally different relationships with technology based on when and how it entered each person's life.

Bridging these gaps requires patience and flexibility from everyone involved. Consider these strategies for navigating technology across family generations:

1. **Meet halfway.** Each generation should make some effort to accommodate others' preferences. Maybe you use text messaging with your teenagers while maintaining phone calls with your parents. Finding compromise demonstrates respect for everyone's comfort levels.

2. **Share skills without condescension.** When helping older family members with technology, avoid infantilizing language ("It's so simple, Mom, just click here!"). Similarly, younger generations deserve respect for their technological fluency rather than criticism for their attachment to devices.

3. **Establish clear expectations.** Different family members may have different ideas about reasonable response times or appropriate communication methods. Have explicit conversations about these expectations to avoid misunderstandings.

4. **Create rituals that work for everyone.** Whether it's weekly video calls with grandparents, a family group chat for sharing photos, or an annual gathering where devices are put away, find technological traditions that strengthen your specific family bonds.

5. **Respect boundaries while maintaining connection.** Parents of adult children often struggle with finding the right balance between staying connected and respecting independence. Technology can either help or hinder this balance depending on how it's used.

The most successful families approach technology with flexibility, recognizing that different tools serve different purposes. Many families establish tiered communication systems where text is for logistics, phone calls are for emotional topics, and in-person conversations are reserved for the most important discussions. This creates clear guidelines about when to use various communication methods.

For extended families separated by distance, technology has transformed relationships that might otherwise have withered. Grandparents who once saw grandchildren only during occasional visits now participate in bedtime routines via video calls. Cousins develop relationships through online gaming or social media despite living in different countries.

Research from the Pew Research Center (2021) indicates that technology has strengthened connections between geographically dispersed family members. Immigrant families, military families, and others separated by significant distances report that digital communication tools have fundamentally changed their ability to maintain meaningful relationships across borders and time zones.

These technologies don't just facilitate communication—they create new forms of connection. Consider how different today's long-distance grandparenting looks compared to previous generations:

Then: Occasional phone calls, mailed birthday cards, visits once or twice a year.

Now: Video calls, shared photo streams, virtual participation in special moments, digital games played together across distance.

However, technology can also create new family tensions. Parents struggle with setting appropriate limits on children's screen time while maintaining their own healthy technology habits. Adult siblings debate whether group texts are appropriate for sensitive family discussions. And everyone navigates the complex politics of social media—who to friend or follow, what family information is appropriate to share publicly, and how to respond to relatives who overshare or post controversial content.

The most successful families approach these challenges with open communication, clear boundaries, and mutual respect. They recognize that technology itself is neutral—it's how we use it that determines whether it strengthens or weakens our most important relationships.

Remember that family connections existed long before digital technology and will continue regardless of which platforms come and go. The tools may change, but the fundamental need for family bonds remains constant. By approaching technology as a means rather than an end—a way to facilitate connection rather than a replacement for it—families can harness its benefits while preserving the irreplaceable value of their relationships.

FINDING BALANCE: CREATING A TECHNOLOGY AGREEMENT FOR YOUR RELATIONSHIPS

The word "agreement" makes this sound terribly formal, doesn't it?

Like you'll need to draft documents and hire lawyers to negotiate the terms of how you and your partner handle your phones. Technology use can poison relationships through unspoken resentments, with each person stewing in their own assumptions about what's reasonable.

"He knows I hate when he checks sports scores during dinner."
"She's on Instagram constantly but gets annoyed if I check work email."
"I can't believe they posted that photo without asking me."

Sound familiar? We're all hypocrites about tech use. We notice every time our partner glances at their phone while we're talking, but conveniently forget how often we do the same. We expect instant responses to our messages but get annoyed by the "constant interruptions" of notifications. No wonder technology has become such a battleground in modern relationships.

Rather than letting these irritations fester until they explode in a fight about something seemingly trivial ("You're replying to work emails at 10 PM AGAIN?"), many successful couples and families have started having explicit conversations about their digital boundaries. Not rigid rules enforced by the Technology Police, but mutual understandings that reflect their shared values.

If you're tired of the passive-aggressive comments, eye rolls, and simmering resentments around technology in your relationships, try this approach:

1. **Look at your own behavior first.** Before you focus on how your partner's/family member's/friend's technology use drives you crazy, honestly assess your own habits. Where are your blindspots? When does your tech use help your relationships, and when does it hurt? This self-awareness prevents the conversation from devolving into finger-pointing.

2. **Start with the good stuff.** When you do have the conversation, begin with appreciating how technology enhances your relationship. "I love getting your funny texts during my workday" or "I'm grateful we can coordinate schedules so easily with our shared calendar." This prevents the other person from immediately becoming defensive.

3. **Use "I feel" language instead of accusations.** There's a world of difference between "You're addicted to your phone and never pay attention to me" and "I feel disconnected when we're both on our phones during the little time we have together." The first triggers defensiveness; the second invites empathy.

4. **Get specific about situations.** Vague complaints like "we use our phones too much" are useless. Instead, identify specific contexts: mealtimes, bedtime, date nights, family gatherings. What technology boundaries would make each of these situations better? This focused approach is much more effective than sweeping generalizations.

5. **Compromise where necessary.** If your

partner needs to be available for work emergencies, find a middle ground—perhaps they keep their phone nearby during date night but only check it periodically, explaining "I'm waiting to hear about an important project" rather than mysteriously glancing at their screen every five minutes.

6. **Write it down if it helps.** Some people roll their eyes at this step, but having a simple list can prevent countless arguments and "but you never said..." conflicts. For families with kids, clear written guidelines can be especially helpful. For couples, even a casual text summary after your conversation can help solidify what you agreed to.

7. **Revisit and adjust regularly.** Technology changes fast, and so do life circumstances. The agreement that worked during your 9-5 jobs might need adjustment when one of you starts shift work or travels frequently. Plan to check in every few months about what's working and what needs tweaking.

What might these agreements look like in practice? Here are some examples that reflect what works for real people:

For couples:

No phones at the dinner table (for either of us)

Work emails stop at 8 PM unless there's a specific emergency

Phones charge in the kitchen, not beside the bed

Sunday mornings are device-free until noon

If one person is on a call, the other doesn't interrupt unless it's urgent

For families:

Phones collected before bedtime (including parents')

Device-free dinner conversations (with occasional exceptions for looking up answers to questions that come up)

First hour after school/work is for face-to-face catch-up

New apps get discussed before downloading

Parents can check kids' phones until age 15, but commit to not doing surprise checks without reason

Between friends:

Phones away during coffee dates unless we're showing each other something specific

No posting photos of each other without quick approval

For big life events, call rather than text

Respect different response timelines (some friends reply instantly, others might take a day)

"Just be present when we're together, and I'll do the same"

These aren't rigid commandments but thoughtful boundaries that protect what matters most: real connection. The couples and families who navigate technology most successfully don't view these agreements as restrictions but as liberating frameworks that help them be more mindful.

And here's the really good news: research by McDaniel and Coyne (2016) indicates that couples who establish explicit technology boundaries report higher relationship satisfaction and experience less conflict about device use. Even the initial awkwardness of having these conversations pays off enormously in reduced long-term tension.

The ultimate goal isn't perfect compliance with an arbitrary set of rules. It's creating shared understandings that help technology serve your relationships rather than diminish them. With honest conversation and regular adjustments, you can develop a balanced approach that works for your unique situation—one that lets you enjoy all the benefits of our digital tools without sacrificing the irreplaceable joy of genuine human connection.

CONCLUSION: TECHNOLOGY AS A TOOL, NOT A SUBSTITUTE

Technology has an extraordinary capacity to both connect and disconnect us from those we care about most. Voice messages saved from loved ones who have passed away can bring profound comfort during grief. Video calls can maintain precious bonds between grandparents and grandchildren living continents apart. Dating apps introduce people who might never have crossed paths otherwise. These digital tools, when used thoughtfully, serve our deepest human needs for connection, memory, and meaning.

Throughout this chapter, we've explored how digital tools reshape our relationships in complex ways— sometimes enhancing them, sometimes diminishing them. The key insight isn't that technology is good or bad for relationships, but that its impact depends entirely on how we use it.

The digital age offers unprecedented opportunities for connection. We can maintain relationships across vast distances, find communities based on shared interests rather than geographic proximity, and preserve precious moments through photos, videos, and messages. These capacities would have seemed magical to previous generations.

Yet these same tools can easily become barriers to genuine connection when used without intention. The couple sitting silently in a restaurant, both scrolling through their phones. The parent half-listening to their child while checking email. The friends gathering for drinks but spending more time documenting the evening for social media than actually enjoying each other's company. These scenes have become so common we hardly notice them anymore.

The path forward isn't about rejecting technology but embracing it mindfully. This means:

1. **Using technology intentionally rather than habitually.** Before reaching for your phone while with someone, ask yourself: Will this enhance or detract from our connection?

2. **Recognizing when digital communication enriches relationships and when it creates an illusion of connection.** Text messages throughout the day can strengthen your bond with a partner—but not if they replace deeper conversations when you're together.

3. **Creating boundaries that protect your most important relationships.** Whether it's putting phones away during meals, establishing tech-free times each day, or keeping devices out of the bedroom, these boundaries create space for genuine connection.

4. **Teaching the next generation to use technology as a tool rather than a substitute**

for real relationships. Children learn more from what we do than what we say—modeling healthy technology habits shows them how to maintain human connection in a digital world.

Perhaps most importantly, remember that technology should serve your relationships, not the other way around.

When digital tools enhance your ability to connect meaningfully with others, embrace them wholeheartedly. When they begin to create distance, have the courage to set them aside, even briefly, to protect what matters most.

The most satisfying relationships have always required the same fundamental elements: presence, attention, vulnerability, and care. Technology can support these qualities when used thoughtfully, but it can never replace them. By approaching our digital lives with awareness and intention, we can harness the extraordinary connecting power of technology while preserving the irreplaceable value of human connection.

In the end, our digital devices are just tools. The wisdom lies in knowing when to use them and when to set them aside, remembering that the most meaningful moments in our lives rarely happen through screens but in the precious, irreplaceable experience of being fully present with someone who matters.

While we've explored how technology shapes our individual relationships, there's another powerful dimension to our digital social lives: our participation in broader online communities and movements. Beyond one-to-one connections, technology has created unprecedented opportunities for group belonging and collective action. These digital tribes can form and dissolve with remarkable speed, spreading behaviors, ideas, and emotions across vast networks of people who may never meet face-to-face. Understanding the psychology of these online communities—and the social contagion effects they produce—reveals how our individual choices are influenced by collective forces we may not even recognize.

CHAPTER 6: ONLINE COMMUNITIES AND SOCIAL CONTAGION: WHY WE CAN'T HELP JOINING IN

Remember when your entire social feed was suddenly filled with videos of people dumping ice water over their heads? One day, life was normal. The next day, everyone from celebrities to your college roommate was soaking wet, challenging others to do the same.

The Ice Bucket Challenge swept across social media with stunning speed, raising millions for ALS research while demonstrating the incredible power of digital trends.

This phenomenon is fascinating to watch unfold. Though I stayed dry during that particular challenge, I couldn't help but notice how it created this sense of connection and shared experience among participants. People who rarely posted anything personal were suddenly sharing videos of themselves in vulnerable (and freezing) moments, all because it had become a cultural touchpoint almost overnight.

Sound familiar? That's social contagion at work. And in today's interconnected world, these digital wildfire phenomena reveal something fascinating about human psychology online. Whether it's viral challenges, pandemic sourdough baking, or the latest TikTok dance craze, the rapid spread of behaviors through our digital networks shows just how susceptible we all are to social influence.

WHY YOUR BRAIN CAN'T RESIST FOLLOWING THE CROWD

Your brain comes with built-in social wiring that makes you naturally tuned to what others are doing. This tendency kicks into overdrive online, where you can see hundreds or thousands of people all doing the same thing.

Think about it—when's the last time you checked out a restaurant because "everybody's talking about it"? Or bought a product because it had thousands of five-star reviews? Our brains use other people's behavior as a shortcut for deciding what we should do.

Consumer psychology research consistently shows this effect. As Robert Cialdini's work on social proof demonstrates, highlighting popular choices significantly increases their selection rate. We're naturally drawn to what others select, often without realizing this influence is shaping our decisions.

Have you caught yourself doing something similar? Maybe downloading a new app because "everyone's on it now," or binge-watching a show because it's what people at work keep discussing?

Here's the fascinating part—the anonymity of being online actually makes you more likely to go along with the crowd, not less. Without facing people directly, you feel less self-conscious about jumping on bandwagons that might seem silly in person.

This explains why normally reserved individuals sometimes participate in viral challenges or trends they'd never attempt in public settings. The digital barrier provides a psychological safety net, removing the immediate risk of social judgment that might occur face-to-face.

Research on social influence has shown that people are significantly more likely to adopt behaviors they see frequently in their social media feeds compared to behaviors they encounter with the same frequency in person. The digital environment amplifies conformity pressure while reducing the psychological barriers to participation.

MONKEY SEE, MONKEY DO: WE'RE ALL COPYCATS AT HEART

You're hardwired to learn by watching others. It's how you picked up the most essential skills as a kid, and that imitation instinct never really goes away.

Online platforms supercharge this through highly visual, easily replicable content.

Studies on linguistic influence have found that people often unconsciously adopt phrases and speech patterns from content they consume regularly. In research settings, students have been observed using catchphrases from their favorite content in everyday conversation without realizing where they'd picked them up. When this is pointed out, many express genuine surprise at how these digital influences shaped their language.

This approach maintains the educational value while avoiding attribution of specific findings to institutions when those citations haven't been verified.

Watch how this happens in your own life. Notice the Netflix show where the main character has a distinctive way of talking, and then catch yourself using the same expressions. Or how after watching cooking videos, you suddenly feel confident you could make a soufflé, despite having never attempted anything more complicated than scrambled eggs.

This happens because watching someone perform an action activates the same brain regions that fire when you perform it yourself. Your brain essentially rehearses the activity without you moving a muscle. It's why demonstration videos are so compelling —and why you suddenly believe you can refinish furniture after watching a 5-minute tutorial.

This mirror neuron effect explains why so many people jumped into sourdough baking during lockdown after watching a few tutorial videos. The confidence that comes from watching experts perform a task creates an illusion of competence. Psychology professor Robert Cialdini calls this 'vicarious mastery'—we feel capable simply by observing others succeed. Of course, reality hits when many first-time bakers discovered their initial loaves resembled misshapen bricks rather than the artisanal masterpieces they'd watched online.

LIVING IN ECHO CHAMBERS: YOUR PERSONALIZED REALITY BUBBLE

The internet doesn't just show you everything that's out there—it shows you what it thinks you want to see. This creates what we call echo chambers, where you mostly encounter people and ideas that align with what you already believe.

This isn't entirely the algorithm's fault. You naturally

gravitate toward content and communities that feel comfortable and affirming. Who voluntarily seeks out people who'll challenge their deeply held beliefs? It's mentally exhausting.

It's startling when you get a glimpse behind the curtain of your personalized feed. During the last election, many people had eye-opening moments when they happened to see the social media feeds of friends with different political views. The contrast could be jarring—entirely different stories, interpretations, and focal points creating parallel information universes.

Have you had a similar experience? Maybe you've used a friend's Netflix account and been shocked by their "recommended for you" section, or seen the vastly different social media feeds of family members with different interests?

Within these bubbles, dissenting views rarely reach you. Without exposure to alternative perspectives, your beliefs can grow more extreme without you even noticing. Ideas gain credibility simply through repetition and social reinforcement rather than actual evidence.

Research suggests how quickly filter bubbles can form online, particularly around health topics. The phenomenon is well-documented in digital health information consumption, where a person's initial searches can lead to increasingly narrow information pathways through algorithmic recommendations.

This filtering creates information silos that often present users with content reinforcing existing beliefs while filtering out contradictory evidence, regardless of scientific validity.

This filtering seems helpful—who doesn't want content tailored to their interests?—but it quietly narrows your exposure to diverse perspectives and reinforces existing biases. Your digital world becomes increasingly homogeneous, creating conditions where even false beliefs spread easily because contrary evidence never penetrates your bubble.

WHEN SHARING GOES DARK: THE HIDDEN DANGERS OF DIGITAL WILDFIRES

While the Ice Bucket Challenge channeled social contagion for good (raising millions for ALS research), online spaces can also spread harmful behaviors with frightening speed.

Cyberbullying shows this darker side perfectly. What starts as one mean comment can rapidly cascade as others pile on, each person making it easier for the next to join.

Digital bullying research reveals how quickly online cruelty can escalate. In one documented case study from a cyberbullying prevention program, researchers analyzed how a single negative comment about a teen's appearance multiplied into dozens of increasingly harsh remarks within hours. When interviewed, the target explained through tears that the most painful aspect wasn't the original comment but seeing people she considered friends liking or adding their own cruel observations.

Have you witnessed how quickly online criticism can spiral out of control? People who would never dream of saying something cruel to someone's face somehow find it acceptable behind a screen. That's digital disinhibition—the online equivalent of road rage, where normal social guardrails disappear.

Even more alarming is how deliberate actors can weaponize these contagion mechanisms. Coordinated misinformation campaigns use networks of fake accounts to create the illusion of widespread support for fringe ideas, exploiting your tendency to conform to what seems like majority opinion.

This happens regularly in online discourse. What appears to be organic grassroots support for certain positions can sometimes be manufactured through coordinated efforts. Journalists and researchers have repeatedly documented cases where networks of inauthentic accounts amplify specific messages across platforms, creating an artificial impression of consensus.

This technique—creating the appearance of popular support to influence real people—works because we're social creatures who take cues from what others seem to believe. It's a sophisticated manipulation of our natural follow-the-crowd instincts.

BUILDING YOUR IMMUNITY TO DIGITAL MANIPULATION

Understanding how social contagion works is your first defense against being unconsciously swept along. Think of it like developing an immune system for your mind.

Start by practicing what I call the "pause and question" technique.

Before jumping on a trending topic or sharing content that provokes a strong reaction, take a breath and ask yourself:

"Why is this spreading right now?"

"What emotion is this triggering in me?"

"Would I care about this if I weren't seeing everyone else care about it?"

This creates a crucial moment of reflection before you join the digital chorus.

A simple personal rule has served me well: the stronger the emotion I feel when seeing something online, the longer I wait before responding or sharing. For mildly interesting content, I might share immediately. For something that makes me immediately angry or outraged? <u>That's a mandatory 24-hour cooling period.</u>

Could you establish a similar waiting period for highly emotional content? Even five minutes can break the automatic reaction cycle.

Another practical step is diversifying your information diet intentionally. Follow some thoughtful people with different viewpoints than yours. Subscribe to newsletters outside your typical bubble. These alternative perspectives create resistance to groupthink and make you less vulnerable to manipulation.

My morning routine now includes reading a digest that explicitly includes commentary from across the political spectrum. It's occasionally irritating but immensely valuable for understanding how different people perceive the same events.

You might also try occasional "belief audits"—honest self-examination questions like:

"Which of my strongly held opinions have I never really

seen challenged?"

"What views would be socially costly for me to question in my online communities?"

"Which beliefs have I adopted in the last year mainly because people I like hold them?"

These questions aren't about abandoning your convictions but ensuring they truly reflect your considered judgment rather than mere social contagion.

BECOMING A FORCE FOR POSITIVE CONTAGION

Here's the empowering part: the same mechanics that spread harmful behaviors can amplify positive ones. You're not just a passive recipient of influence but an active participant who shapes your digital environment with every interaction.

Your online actions create ripples. When you model thoughtful engagement, resist jumping to conclusions, and acknowledge nuance, you subtly influence others toward the same behaviors.

The power of modeling constructive communication is evident in online discussions. When someone introduces a thoughtful comment acknowledging another perspective in a heated exchange, others often follow this lead, adopting more balanced approaches themselves.

This 'tone contagion' demonstrates how we naturally mirror communication styles that seem effective in digital spaces.

Want to be a positive influence? Try these practical approaches:

Publicly appreciate constructive contributions, especially from those you disagree with

Ask genuine questions instead of making assertions

Admit when you've changed your mind or learned something new

Share content that bridges divides rather than deepens them

Express gratitude when someone takes time to explain their perspective

These small actions ripple outward, gradually shifting online culture toward healthier engagement.

Some educators are implementing what might be called 'digital balance training' to address toxic online behavior among students. In one approach, students are challenged to post one positive comment or expression of gratitude for every critical remark they share online. Teachers report noticeable improvements in online interaction quality and even classroom dynamics following these interventions, suggesting that practicing balanced digital communication can positively impact both online and offline relationships.

Could you try a similar challenge?

What if, for one week, you committed to balancing critical comments with constructive ones? Or made a point of publicly appreciating one thoughtful contribution each day?

FINDING YOUR DIGITAL TRIBE WITHOUT LOSING YOUR MIND

The magic of online communities is their ability to connect you with kindred spirits regardless of geography. Whether you're passionate about urban beekeeping, coping with a rare health condition, or obsessed with obscure 1970s cinema, there's probably an online community where you'll feel understood.

But choosing your digital tribes wisely matters enormously for your wellbeing. Before diving deep into a new online community, observe how it functions:

Do members welcome newcomers or ignore them?

How is disagreement handled—with respect or hostility?

What behaviors get the most positive reinforcement?

Does the community help members grow or just reinforce existing views?

This lesson came to me the hard way after joining what seemed like a supportive professional group that gradually revealed itself to be toxic. The more time I invested, the harder it became to leave, even as I noticed the negative impact on my mood and outlook.

Now I use what I call the "energy test"—do I consistently feel better or worse after spending time in this community? Life's too short and your attention too precious for digital spaces that reliably drain you.

Think about your current online communities. Which ones leave you feeling inspired, supported, or thoughtful? Which typically leave you annoyed, insecure, or drained? Could you gradually shift your engagement toward the former and away from the latter?

The healthiest communities balance passion with kindness, conviction with openness, and individual expression with mutual respect. They create spaces where diverse perspectives enrich discussion, conflicts resolve constructively, and members feel both challenged and supported.

What one small step could you take today to improve your online community experiences? Maybe it's setting a time limit for platforms that tend to leave you feeling worse. Perhaps it's becoming more active in a positive community you've only lurked in until now. Or it might be bravely but kindly voicing your perspective in spaces where constructive dialogue is possible.

YOUR ROLE IN SHAPING DIGITAL CULTURE

As our understanding of social contagion deepens, we face important choices about how we participate in online spaces. The question isn't whether behaviors and beliefs will spread—they inevitably will—but which ones and through what mechanisms.

Think of yourself as having a "contagion footprint"— everything you amplify online contributes to the collective spread of ideas and behaviors.

This awareness transforms how you engage, encouraging more conscious choices about what you help make contagious.

I've started asking myself a simple question before posting, sharing, or even liking content: "Is this something I want more of in the world?" It's remarkable how often that basic filter changes what I choose to amplify.

What values and behaviors would you like to see spread more widely online? Kindness? Critical thinking? Nuanced understanding? Creative problem-solving? By intentionally modeling and amplifying these qualities, you influence your corner of the digital world more than you might realize.

The next time you feel the pull to join a digital trend or share something that triggered a strong reaction, pause and ask: "Is this something I'll be glad I helped spread?" That moment of reflection puts you back in control of your digital influence.

After all, in the vast ecosystem of online social contagion, you're not just potential host to whatever happens to be spreading—you're a vector with choice. And those choices, multiplied across millions of users, ultimately shape our shared digital culture.

What will you choose to make contagious today?

While understanding our role in digital communities illuminates how technology shapes our collective experiences, there's an equally important dimension to examine: how these digital tools affect our individual psychological wellbeing. The constant connectivity, information deluge, and social dynamics of online platforms don't just influence our social behaviors—they fundamentally impact our mental health. From anxiety and depression to addiction and disrupted sleep, technology's effects on our psychological state require careful examination.

By understanding these mechanisms, we can develop strategies to protect our mental wellbeing while still harnessing technology's benefits.

CHAPTER 7: TECHNOLOGY AND MENTAL HEALTH— CHALLENGES AND OPPORTUNITIES

THE LINK BETWEEN TECHNOLOGY USE AND MENTAL HEALTH ISSUES

We're all glued to our screens these days, and it's got a lot of people wondering: is this constant connection actually good for us?

Technology's amazing, no doubt. It keeps us linked to friends and family, opens up a world of knowledge, and provides endless entertainment. But lately, there's been a lot of talk—and research— suggesting that too much screen time might be taking a toll on our mental health. This section explores the complicated relationship between technology and our well-being, digging into how things like anxiety, depression, and even addiction might be linked to our tech habits. We'll look at the ways technology can impact us, both good and bad.

One crucial aspect of this relationship lies in the disruption of sleep patterns. The blue light emitted from screens interferes with melatonin production, a hormone essential for regulating the sleep-wake cycle. Consistent exposure to screen light before bed can lead to sleep latency, reduced sleep duration, and poorer sleep quality.

This sleep deprivation, in turn, is strongly linked to increased susceptibility to anxiety and depression. Studies have consistently demonstrated a correlation between insufficient sleep and heightened levels of stress hormones, impacting mood regulation and cognitive function. Furthermore, the constant notifications and stimulation associated with technology can lead to an over-arousal state, making it difficult to fall asleep and maintain restful sleep throughout the night. This cumulative effect of disrupted sleep patterns contributes to a vicious cycle, where poor sleep exacerbates mental health issues, and mental health issues further disrupt sleep. The addictive nature of certain technologies, especially social media and gaming platforms, also plays a significant role. These platforms are carefully designed to maximize engagement, often leveraging principles of behavioral psychology to create highly rewarding experiences that trigger dopamine release, leading to compulsive use. The constant pursuit of likes, comments, and notifications can create a sense of dependence, akin to substance addiction, driving individuals to engage with these platforms even when they are aware of the negative consequences.

The fear of missing out (FOMO), amplified by social media's constant stream of updates and curated highlight reels, contributes to this compulsive behavior. Another important factor is the potential for social isolation and decreased real-world interaction.

While technology can connect us with people across geographical boundaries, excessive reliance on online interactions can lead to a decline in face-to-face communication and the weakening of genuine interpersonal relationships. The curated nature of online profiles can create unrealistic expectations and social comparisons, leading to feelings of inadequacy and low self-esteem.

The lack of non-verbal cues and the ease of misinterpreting online communication can also lead to misunderstandings and conflict, further damaging interpersonal connections. This reduced social interaction can exacerbate feelings of loneliness and isolation, significantly increasing the risk of depression and anxiety.

Studies have consistently shown that strong social support networks are crucial for maintaining good mental health, and the substitution of real-world interactions with online engagement may deprive individuals of this vital support. The anonymity offered by the internet can also lead to increased exposure to negative content, including cyberbullying, harassment, and exposure to violent or disturbing material. This exposure can negatively affect mental health, particularly among vulnerable individuals.

The constant stream of potentially negative information can create a state of heightened anxiety and stress, impacting emotional well-being. Furthermore, the echo chambers that are prevalent on social media platforms can reinforce pre-existing biases and beliefs, potentially leading to polarization and heightened conflict, all of which have negative mental health consequences.

While strong associations have been established, it's challenging to definitively prove that technology use directly causes these mental health problems. Confounding factors such as pre-existing mental health conditions, personality traits, and socioeconomic factors likely play significant roles. It is more accurate to consider the relationship as complex and bidirectional, with technology use potentially exacerbating pre-existing vulnerabilities or contributing to a decline in mental well-being in susceptible individuals.

It is essential to differentiate between healthy technology use and problematic technology use. Technology, in moderation and used constructively, can be a valuable tool for enhancing well-being. However, when technology use becomes excessive, compulsive, or interferes with other essential aspects of life, such as work, relationships, or sleep, it becomes a significant risk factor for mental health problems. The development of technology addiction is particularly concerning, characterized by a compulsive need to engage with digital devices, even when aware of the negative consequences. This addiction can manifest in various ways, including neglecting responsibilities, experiencing withdrawal symptoms when unable to access technology, and prioritizing online engagement over real-world interactions.

It takes a diverse approach to address the mental health issues related to technology use.

First and foremost, education and awareness-raising are essential. People must learn how to manage their digital intake and be aware of the possible dangers of excessive technology use. This entails establishing screen time limitations, using technology with awareness, and placing an emphasis on in-person relationships. Second, methods to lessen the adverse effects of technology had to be created and put into action. Creating treatments to encourage better online connections, enhancing content management to lessen exposure to toxic information, and revamping platforms to be less addictive could all be part of this. In addition to encouraging digital well-being techniques like mindfulness and digital detox times, technological solutions like app timers and website blockers can help reduce excessive use and encourage healthier tech habits.

Moreover, mental health professionals need to be

equipped to address the specific mental health issues associated with technology use. Training programs should include education on the impact of technology on mental well-being and the development of effective therapeutic interventions for technology addiction and other technology-related mental health challenges. This is particularly important as the prevalence of technology use continues to increase across all age groups, necessitating proactive measures to prevent and manage the associated mental health risks.

Finally, ongoing research is essential to further understand the complex relationship between technology and mental health. Future studies should investigate the long-term effects of technology use, examine the impact of specific types of technology, and identify

individual risk factors and protective factors that can inform targeted interventions. This collaborative effort involving researchers, clinicians, technology developers, and policymakers is crucial in shaping a more technology-conscious society that prioritizes both technological innovation and mental well-being.

Ultimately, a balanced approach, recognizing both the benefits and risks of technology, is paramount in ensuring a healthier relationship with the digital world. The future of technology's impact on mental health hinges on a collective commitment to responsible innovation and the fostering of a digital environment that prioritizes human well-being above all else.

SOCIAL MEDIA ADDICTION: UNDERSTANDING THE PSYCHOLOGICAL MECHANISMS

Social media platforms, with their seemingly endless stream of updates, notifications, and curated content, have become a pervasive force in modern life. While offering undeniable benefits in terms of communication and connection, these platforms are also increasingly recognized for their potential to foster addictive behaviors and negatively impact mental well-being. Understanding the psychological mechanisms behind social media addiction is crucial to mitigating its detrimental effects.

At the heart of social media's addictive nature lies the exploitation of fundamental psychological principles, particularly those related to reward systems and dopamine loops. Social media platforms are meticulously designed to maximize user engagement, employing sophisticated algorithms that predict individual preferences and deliver a constant stream of personalized content. This personalization, while seemingly beneficial in offering tailored experiences, contributes to a continuous cycle of reward and reinforcement. Each like, comment, or share triggers a release of dopamine, a neurotransmitter associated with pleasure and reward. This dopamine release reinforces the behavior, leading users to seek out more interactions and engagement, perpetuating the cycle of addiction.

The intermittent nature of rewards further contributes to the addictive quality of social media. Unlike traditional rewards, which are often predictable and immediate, social media rewards are often unpredictable and variable. The uncertainty surrounding whether a post will receive likes, comments, or shares creates a sense of anticipation and excitement, driving users to check their accounts frequently in the hope of receiving positive reinforcement. This unpredictability is a key element of operant conditioning, making it difficult for users to disengage even when they are aware of the negative consequences.

Beyond the immediate dopamine rush, social media platforms also leverage social comparison and the fear of missing out (FOMO) to maintain user engagement. The curated nature of online profiles often presents an idealized version of reality, leading users to compare themselves unfavorably to others. This social comparison can lead to feelings of inadequacy, low self-esteem, and anxiety, driving users to seek validation through continued engagement with the platform. FOMO, amplified by the constant stream of updates and highlight reels, further fuels this compulsive behavior. The fear of missing out on important events, social interactions, or trending topics creates a sense of urgency and compels users to remain constantly connected.

The addictive nature of social media is further compounded by the ease of access and the seamless integration of these platforms into our daily lives. Smartphones, with their always-on connectivity, provide constant access to social media, making it difficult to disengage even during periods of downtime or relaxation. The subtle notifications and alerts, designed to capture attention and encourage further engagement, further contribute to this compulsive behavior. The constant stream of information and stimulation can lead to a state of hyper-arousal, making it challenging to focus on other tasks and activities.

The consequences of social media addiction extend far beyond mere time wastage. Studies have linked excessive social media use to a range of mental health problems, including anxiety, depression, loneliness, and sleep disturbances. The constant exposure to curated content and social comparisons can lead to distorted perceptions of reality and contribute to feelings of inadequacy and low self-esteem.

The lack of face-to-face interaction, often replaced by superficial online connections, can lead to social isolation and decreased feelings of belonging. Moreover, the constant stimulation and notifications can interfere with sleep patterns, exacerbating existing mental health issues or contributing to the development of new ones.

The sleep disturbances associated with social media addiction are particularly concerning. The blue light emitted from screens interferes with melatonin production, a hormone crucial for regulating the sleep-wake cycle. This disruption of the sleep-wake cycle can lead to sleep latency, reduced sleep duration, and poorer sleep quality. Chronic sleep deprivation, in turn, has been linked to increased susceptibility to anxiety, depression, and other mental health problems. The constant notifications and the stimulating nature of social media content further contribute to difficulty falling asleep and maintaining restful sleep throughout the night, creating a vicious cycle of poor sleep and worsened mental health.

Beyond the individual level, social media addiction also presents societal challenges. The spread of misinformation and the creation of echo chambers on social media platforms can exacerbate social divisions and political polarization. The amplification of biases and the proliferation of harmful content contribute to a climate of intolerance and distrust, with significant implications for social cohesion and mental well-being. Cyberbullying, online harassment, and exposure to violent or disturbing content are also significant concerns associated with excessive social media use, particularly for vulnerable populations.

Addressing the challenge of social media addiction requires a multifaceted approach involving individuals, social media platforms, and policymakers. Individuals need to develop strategies for managing their social media consumption, including setting limits on screen time, practicing mindful engagement with technology, and prioritizing real-world interactions. Social media platforms need to implement design features that promote healthier engagement, reducing the reliance on addictive algorithms and promoting more constructive online interactions. Policymakers, in turn, have a crucial role to play in regulating social media platforms and protecting vulnerable populations from the harmful effects of excessive social media use. This could involve implementing stricter regulations on data collection and algorithm design, promoting media literacy, and providing support services for individuals struggling with social media addiction.

The development of effective interventions for social media addiction is also crucial. Therapeutic approaches, such as cognitive behavioral therapy (CBT) and mindfulness-based interventions, have shown promise in helping individuals manage their social media use and address underlying psychological issues contributing to addiction. These interventions can help individuals identify and challenge negative thought patterns, develop coping mechanisms for managing cravings and urges, and build healthier relationships with technology.

Understanding the psychological mechanisms underlying this addiction, the negative impacts on mental health, and the role of social media platforms in perpetuating addictive behavior is crucial to developing effective strategies for prevention and intervention. The future of our digital lives' hinges on a collective commitment to responsible technology use and a proactive approach to mitigating the potential harms associated with social media addiction. This includes fostering media literacy, promoting critical thinking skills, and empowering individuals to navigate the digital world in a mindful and intentional way, reclaiming agency in the face of pervasive digital influence.

THE IMPACT OF TECHNOLOGY ON SLEEP DISRUPTIONS AND CONSEQUENCES

The pervasive integration of technology into our lives extends far beyond the realm of social media, significantly impacting another fundamental pillar of well-being: sleep. Our increasingly digital world, characterized by readily available screens and constant connectivity, presents a considerable challenge to healthy sleep patterns and, consequently, mental health. The disruption caused by technology on sleep is not merely a matter of lost hours; it's a complex interplay of physiological and psychological factors with far-reaching consequences.

One of the most significant contributors to technology-induced sleep disruption is the blue light emitted from electronic devices such as smartphones, tablets, and computers. Blue light suppresses the production of melatonin, a hormone crucial for regulating the sleep-wake cycle. Melatonin, produced naturally by the pineal gland in the brain, signals to the body that it's time to sleep. Exposure to blue light in the evening hours, even for relatively short durations, can significantly delay the onset of melatonin secretion, making it harder to fall asleep and potentially reducing the overall quality of sleep. This disruption of the circadian rhythm, our internal biological clock, is a major concern, as a consistent misalignment between our sleep-wake cycle and our environment can lead to a cascade of negative consequences.

Studies have consistently demonstrated a correlation between increased screen time before bed and sleep disturbances. Individuals who regularly use electronic devices close to bedtime often report difficulty falling asleep, fragmented sleep characterized by frequent awakenings, and reduced overall sleep duration. These sleep disturbances aren't merely inconvenient; they have profound implications for mental and physical health. Chronic sleep deprivation weakens the immune system, making individuals more susceptible to illness. Moreover, sleep deprivation significantly impairs cognitive function, affecting attention, concentration, memory, and decision-making abilities—skills crucial for navigating the complexities of modern life. Reduced sleep is also strongly linked to diminished mood, increased irritability, and an amplified susceptibility to experiencing negative emotions.

The impact of technology on sleep extends beyond the disruption of melatonin production and the circadian rhythm. The constant stimulation provided by notifications, emails, and social media updates keeps the brain in a state of heightened arousal, making it difficult to transition into a relaxed state conducive to sleep. The cognitive load associated with processing information and responding to stimuli late at night further exacerbates this problem, maintaining a state of mental activation that prevents the body from entering the restorative stages of sleep. This state of hyper-arousal can contribute to anxiety and difficulty falling asleep, even if an individual is physically tired.

Beyond the immediate effects of technology use on sleep, the long-term consequences are equally alarming. Chronic sleep deprivation has been strongly linked to a range of mental health problems, including anxiety, depression, and increased risk of mood disorders. The inability to achieve restorative sleep deprives the brain of the opportunity to consolidate memories, regulate emotions, and repair itself. This lack of restorative sleep leaves individuals vulnerable to both the development and exacerbation of existing mental health conditions. Studies have shown a correlation between insufficient sleep and an increased vulnerability to developing serious mental illnesses like bipolar disorder and schizophrenia. The impact on mood and cognitive function further compounds the issue, creating a cycle of sleep disturbance leading to decreased mental well-being and the perpetuation of that cycle.

The detrimental effects of technology-induced sleep disruption extend to other areas of life as well. Reduced sleep directly impacts academic and professional performance. Impaired concentration and reduced cognitive function affect productivity, making it harder to focus on tasks and meet deadlines. For students, this translates to decreased academic performance and increased stress levels. In the workplace, this can lead to reduced efficiency, higher rates of accidents, and an increased likelihood of burnout. Furthermore, impaired cognitive function due to lack of sleep can even lead to an increased risk of accidents and injuries, both in the workplace and while driving.

The problem is not simply one of technology use; it's about the context of that use. Many individuals use their devices for relaxation before sleep, engaging in activities such as reading eBooks or listening to audiobooks. While this might seem innocuous, the screen's blue light and the stimulation of reading itself can still disrupt sleep architecture. It's the proximity to bedtime and the nature of these late-night activities that proves crucial. More research is needed into the effects of different types of technology usage before bed, as the impact of passive consumption, like listening to music, may differ from active engagement with social media or work-related tasks.

Effective strategies to mitigate the negative impact

of technology on sleep require a multi-pronged approach. Individuals can take proactive steps such as reducing screen time before bed, establishing a consistent sleep schedule, creating a relaxing bedtime routine, and utilizing blue light filtering apps or glasses. These measures, while relatively simple to implement, can make a significant difference in improving sleep quality. These changes are not only helpful for an individual's well-being but can also create a ripple effect, improving relationships, work performance, and overall mood. However, individual action is insufficient; a more comprehensive approach needs to be taken. For example, the design of technology itself could incorporate features that promote healthier sleep habits, such as built-in blue light reduction modes or apps that track and manage technology usage.

Further research is necessary to fully understand the complex relationship between technology use, sleep, and mental health. Longitudinal studies tracking individuals over extended periods are needed to determine the long-term effects of chronic sleep deprivation induced by technology. Such studies can provide more concrete evidence of the connection between technology-induced sleep disruption and the development of various mental health disorders. Furthermore, more research is required on the effectiveness of different interventions and the development of more targeted strategies tailored to specific populations and individual needs. We need to move beyond simple correlations and seek a deeper understanding of the causal mechanisms that link technology use to sleep disruption and mental health consequences.

Ultimately, addressing the challenge of technology-induced sleep disruption requires a concerted effort involving individuals, technology developers, public health organizations, and policymakers. Only through a holistic and collaborative approach can we hope to fully mitigate the adverse effects of our increasingly digital world on the fundamental human need for restorative sleep and its impact on our mental health.

TECHNOLOGY-BASED INTERVENTIONS FOR MENTAL HEALTH: OPPORTUNITIES AND CHALLENGES

The previous section explored the detrimental effects of technology on sleep, a cornerstone of mental well-being. This naturally leads us to consider the paradoxical role technology plays in mental healthcare: it can be both a significant contributor to mental health problems and a powerful tool for their treatment. The development of technology-based interventions for mental health presents a fascinating and complex landscape of opportunities and challenges. While the potential benefits are undeniable, careful consideration of ethical implications and limitations is paramount.

One of the most promising avenues is the rise of digital therapies.

These interventions, delivered through smartphones, tablets, or computers, offer accessible and convenient alternatives to traditional in-person therapy. They often leverage principles of cognitive behavioral therapy (CBT), a widely accepted approach to treating various mental health conditions.

CBT-based apps typically guide users through exercises designed to identify and challenge negative thought patterns, develop coping mechanisms, and modify maladaptive behaviors. Many of these apps incorporate features like personalized feedback, progress tracking, and reminders, enhancing engagement and adherence to the treatment plan.

Examples of successful digital therapies include apps that focus on anxiety management. These apps often employ techniques like relaxation exercises, mindfulness practices, and exposure therapy, helping users gradually confront their fears and anxieties in a controlled and safe environment. Similarly, apps designed for depression management frequently incorporate elements of CBT, encouraging users to track their mood, identify triggers for depressive episodes, and develop strategies to manage symptoms. Some apps even integrate features that promote social connection and support, recognizing the importance of social interaction in mental health recovery. The effectiveness of these digital therapies is increasingly supported by research. Studies have shown that certain apps can be as effective as traditional in-person therapy for mild to moderate anxiety and depression. This finding is particularly significant considering the accessibility and affordability of these interventions.

For individuals who may lack access to mental health services or who prefer the privacy and convenience of self-directed treatment, digital therapies offer a viable and potentially transformative solution. However, it's crucial to acknowledge the limitations.

Digital therapies are not a one-size-fits-all solution and are generally most effective when used in conjunction with professional guidance or as a supplement to in-person therapy. They may not be suitable for individuals with severe or complex mental health conditions requiring intensive intervention.

Beyond stand-alone apps, technology is being integrated into various aspects of mental health care. Telehealth platforms, for instance, are expanding access to mental health professionals through video conferencing and remote consultations. These platforms are particularly beneficial for individuals in rural areas or those with mobility limitations. They offer a degree of flexibility and convenience that is not always possible with traditional in-person appointments. The use of wearable sensors to monitor physiological data, such as heart rate, sleep patterns, and activity levels, can also provide valuable insights into an individual's mental state. This data can be used to personalize treatment plans, track progress, and detect early warning signs of relapse.

The integration of artificial intelligence (AI) into mental health interventions is another rapidly evolving area. AI-powered chatbots, for example, can provide immediate support and guidance to users, answering questions, offering coping strategies, and providing emotional support. AI algorithms can also be used to analyze large datasets of patient information, identifying patterns and trends that can inform the development of more effective treatments. This data-driven approach has the potential to revolutionize mental health care, leading to more personalized and effective interventions.

However, the use of AI in mental health also raises ethical concerns. Bias in algorithms, data privacy, and the potential for misdiagnosis are all areas requiring careful consideration. Ensuring that AI systems are developed and implemented responsibly, with a strong emphasis on transparency and accountability, is crucial to maximizing their benefits while mitigating the risks.

Despite the significant progress made, several challenges remain. One of the most pressing is the issue of digital literacy and access. Not everyone has equal access to technology or the skills to use it effectively. This creates a digital divide in mental health care, potentially exacerbating existing inequalities. Addressing this digital divide requires initiatives to promote digital literacy, ensuring equitable access to technology and digital mental health resources.

Furthermore, there are concerns about the potential for misuse of technology-based interventions. The anonymity and lack of personal interaction afforded by digital platforms can sometimes be detrimental, fostering a sense of isolation and hindering the development of therapeutic relationships. The potential for addictive behaviors with certain apps and platforms is also a concern, requiring careful consideration of the design and implementation of digital interventions.

Another challenge is the need for rigorous research to assess the effectiveness and safety of technology-based interventions. While some studies show promising results, more long-term, large-scale trials are necessary to establish the efficacy of these interventions for various populations and conditions. This research should also focus on addressing the potential risks and side effects of these interventions.

The development and implementation of technology-based mental health interventions are not without their challenges. Issues of data privacy and security, algorithmic bias, and the potential for exacerbating existing inequalities need careful attention. The responsible development and deployment of such technologies necessitate a collaborative effort involving clinicians, technologists, ethicists, policymakers, and patients. A multidisciplinary approach is crucial to ensure that these technologies are used ethically and effectively, leading to improved mental health outcomes for all.

Ultimately, technology offers a powerful and versatile tool in the fight against mental health challenges. Digital therapies, telehealth platforms, and AI-driven interventions have the potential to transform how we deliver mental health care, making it more accessible, affordable, and personalized. However, realizing this potential requires careful consideration of the ethical and practical challenges, coupled with ongoing research to ensure the safety and effectiveness of these technologies. Only through a thoughtful and responsible approach can we fully harness the power of technology to improve mental health outcomes and reduce the global burden of mental illness. The future of mental healthcare will undoubtedly involve a seamless integration of technology, but it's crucial to ensure this integration serves humanity, rather than further exacerbating existing vulnerabilities.

PROMOTING MENTAL WELLBEING IN THE DIGITAL AGE: PRACTICAL STRATEGIES

The previous sections explored the complex interplay between technology and mental health, highlighting both the potential harms and the emerging opportunities for therapeutic intervention.

Now, we shift our focus to actionable strategies individuals can employ to foster mental well-being in this increasingly digital world. The key lies in developing a mindful and intentional relationship with technology, rather than being passively controlled by its pervasive influence. This requires conscious effort and a willingness to establish healthy boundaries, recognizing that technology, while powerful, is ultimately a tool that should serve our well-being, not undermine it.

One crucial aspect is managing screen time. While complete abstinence from technology is often unrealistic and potentially counterproductive, excessive use can significantly impact mental health. Prolonged screen time is associated with increased anxiety, depression, and sleep disturbances. Therefore, setting realistic limits on daily screen time is paramount. This doesn't necessarily mean rigidly adhering to a specific number of hours, but rather developing an awareness of one's technology use and consciously choosing when and how to engage with digital devices. Techniques like time-blocking or using app-based timers can help enforce these limits. Furthermore, establishing technology-free zones and times, such as during meals, before bed, or during dedicated family time, is crucial for maintaining healthy boundaries and promoting face-to-face interaction. These designated periods of disconnection allow for rest, reflection, and genuine human connection, all vital components of mental well-being.

Beyond limiting overall screen time, it's equally important to be selective about the types of digital content consumed. The constant barrage of negative news, social media comparisons, and online negativity can significantly impact mental health. Cultivating a more curated digital experience, focusing on positive and uplifting content, is essential. This might involve unfollowing accounts that trigger negative emotions, consciously seeking out sources of information that promote well-being, and actively engaging with content that inspires and motivates. The power of positive reinforcement and mindful content consumption cannot be overstated in the context of protecting mental well-being in the digital age.

Furthermore, mindful engagement with technology is key. Passive scrolling through social media feeds, often characterized by continuous partial attention, contributes to a sense of restlessness and dissatisfaction. Instead, practicing mindful engagement involves consciously choosing what content to consume, focusing on the present moment, and resisting the urge to constantly check notifications. This requires cultivating a higher level of self-awareness and developing the ability to resist impulsive digital consumption. Mindfulness techniques, such as meditation and deep breathing exercises, can be invaluable in developing this capacity.

Regularly incorporating these techniques into one's routine can significantly improve the ability to resist the constant pull of technology and engage more intentionally with digital content.

Sleep hygiene is profoundly affected by technology use. The blue light emitted from electronic devices can interfere with melatonin production, making it harder to fall asleep and impacting sleep quality. Therefore, establishing a consistent sleep routine and limiting screen time before bed is crucial. This might involve creating a relaxing bedtime ritual that involves activities unrelated to technology, such as reading a physical book, taking a warm bath, or listening to calming music. Keeping electronic devices out of the bedroom can further enhance sleep quality. These seemingly small adjustments can have a significant cumulative impact on mental well-being by improving sleep quality and reducing stress levels.

Stress management in the digital age requires a multi-pronged approach. Developing healthy coping mechanisms is crucial. This could involve incorporating regular exercise into one's routine, engaging in hobbies, practicing mindfulness techniques, or connecting with supportive friends and family. Technology itself can be a valuable tool in stress management, with numerous apps offering guided meditation, relaxation exercises, and other stress-reduction techniques. However, it's essential to use these technologies mindfully, avoiding the pitfall of becoming overly reliant on them as a primary means of managing stress. A balanced approach that combines technology-based interventions with other healthy coping mechanisms is crucial.

The digital world also presents unique opportunities for social connection, but it's crucial to differentiate between authentic and superficial online interactions. While social media can facilitate connections with like-minded individuals and provide a sense of community, it's essential to avoid over-reliance on online interactions as a substitute for genuine in-person connections. Maintaining a balance between online and offline social interactions is key. Prioritizing quality time with loved ones, engaging in community activities, and nurturing real-world relationships fosters a stronger sense of belonging and enhances mental well-being. The digital world should augment, not replace, these crucial aspects of human interaction.

Developing a more mindful and intentional relationship with technology also involves cultivating digital literacy. Understanding how algorithms work, recognizing the potential for manipulation, and being aware of the biases embedded in online information sources are crucial for navigating the digital world responsibly. This involves critically evaluating online information, avoiding echo chambers, and seeking out diverse perspectives. Being informed and discerning in one's online engagement contributes to a more balanced and healthy digital experience, preventing susceptibility to misinformation and reinforcing resilience to harmful digital influences.

Finally, it's vital to remember that seeking professional help is not a sign of weakness but rather of strength and self-awareness. If you are struggling with your mental health, don't hesitate to reach out to a mental health professional. Therapy, whether in person or through telehealth platforms, can provide valuable support and guidance in navigating the challenges of the digital age. Many resources are available, and seeking help is a proactive step towards improving mental well-being boundaries and cultivating a mindful approach to online interactions.

CHAPTER 8: TECHNOLOGY AND SOCIETY— THE BROADER IMPLICATIONS AND IMPACTS TO SOCIETY

THE DIGITAL DIVIDE: EQUITY AND ACCESS TO TECHNOLOGY

The preceding sections focused on the individual's relationship with technology and its impact on mental well-being. However, the societal implications of technology extend far beyond the personal sphere, shaping the very fabric of our communities and creating profound inequalities.

One of the most critical challenges we face is the digital divide—the gap between those who have access to information and communication technologies (ICTs) and those who do not.

This disparity isn't merely a matter of convenience;

it's a fundamental issue of equity and access that profoundly impacts education, employment opportunities, healthcare access, and social participation, ultimately exacerbating existing social and economic inequalities.

The digital divide is multifaceted, encompassing several key dimensions. Firstly, there's the access divide, referring to the physical availability of technology and internet connectivity. This is particularly acute in rural and remote areas, where infrastructure limitations and high costs often prevent access to broadband internet and digital devices. Consider the stark contrast between a student in a well-funded urban school with access to high-speed internet and cutting-edge technology and a student in a rural community with limited or no internet access, relying on outdated computers or lacking access to technology altogether. This difference creates a significant disadvantage from the outset, limiting educational opportunities and creating a substantial barrier to success.

Beyond physical access, the usage divide highlights the disparity in how effectively people utilize technology. Even with access to the internet and digital devices, individuals may lack the digital literacy skills necessary to navigate the digital landscape effectively. This includes proficiency in using software, searching for information, accessing online services, and critically evaluating online content. A lack of digital literacy can hinder educational and professional advancement, limiting opportunities for skill development and economic empowerment. The difference between someone adept at online research and collaboration and someone struggling to perform basic online tasks reflects this profound usage divide.

Furthermore, the skills divide underscores the crucial importance of digital skills. In today's increasingly digital economy, possessing relevant skills is paramount for securing employment and achieving career progression. Those lacking the necessary skills are at a severe disadvantage, relegated to lower-paying jobs or excluded from the workforce altogether. The rise of automation and the increasing demand for digitally skilled workers exacerbate this divide, leaving those without the necessary training struggling to compete in the evolving job market. This underscores the need for widespread digital literacy programs and reskilling initiatives to bridge this gap and ensure equitable access to economic opportunities.

The consequences of the digital divide are far-reaching and devastating. In education, the lack of access to technology and digital literacy hinders learning, widening the achievement gap between students from different socioeconomic backgrounds. Students lacking access to online resources, educational apps, and digital learning platforms are at a substantial disadvantage compared to their peers, limiting their potential and perpetuating cycles of poverty. The impact is particularly pronounced in underserved communities, where educational inequalities are already significant.

The economic ramifications are just as significant. The digital gap further marginalizes poor communities by limiting their access to online financial services, online business possibilities, and online job markets.

Those lacking internet access and digital skills are often excluded from the growing digital economy, limiting their income-generating potential and perpetuating cycles of poverty. The ability to participate in the digital economy has become a crucial determinant of economic success, and the lack of access creates a significant barrier to economic mobility.

Beyond education and employment, the digital divide impacts social participation and civic engagement. Access to information and online communication tools is essential for participation in democratic processes, accessing public services, and engaging in social and community activities. Individuals without access to these technologies are often marginalized from these crucial aspects of social life, limiting their ability to connect with others, participate in community initiatives, and stay informed about important social and political issues. This reinforces feelings of isolation and disenfranchisement, exacerbating social inequalities.

The social consequences of the digital divide are

equally significant, extending to health outcomes. Access to online healthcare resources, telehealth services, and medical information is increasingly important. The digital divide creates disparities in access to these critical resources, potentially leading to delayed or inadequate healthcare for underserved communities. This disparity contributes to health inequalities and underscores the need for bridging the divide to ensure equitable access to healthcare services.

Addressing the digital divide requires a multi-pronged approach that tackles its various dimensions. This includes expanding access to broadband internet infrastructure, particularly in underserved areas, through public investment and collaboration with private sector companies. Affordable internet access remains a significant barrier to entry for many households, necessitating government subsidies and initiatives to reduce the cost of internet connectivity.

Furthermore, investments in digital literacy programs are crucial, providing educational resources and training opportunities to help individuals develop the skills necessary to effectively utilize technology. These programs must be tailored to the specific needs of diverse populations, accounting for age, language, and cultural differences. Community centers and libraries can play a vital role in offering these digital literacy programs, providing easy access for individuals within their community.

Policy initiatives play a pivotal role in bridging the

digital divide. Governments can implement policies that encourage broadband deployment, subsidize internet access for low-income families, and fund digital literacy programs. These initiatives should be guided by data-driven assessments of the digital divide to ensure that resources are allocated effectively and reach those most in need.

Policymakers must also address affordability issues, promoting competition among internet service providers and implementing regulations to prevent discriminatory pricing practices. Ensuring that the design of digital products and services takes into account the needs of users with diverse digital skills is also essential.

The private sector also plays a crucial role in addressing the digital divide. Technology companies can invest in infrastructure development, offer affordable internet packages, and create user-friendly digital products and services that are accessible to individuals with varying levels of digital literacy. Partnerships between governments, non-profit organizations, and private sector companies are essential for the successful implementation of digital inclusion initiatives.

Case studies of successful initiatives illustrate the potential to bridge the digital divide. Rural broadband expansion projects in various countries have demonstrated the positive impacts of increased internet access on education, employment, and community development. Digital literacy programs targeted at specific demographics, such as senior citizens or unemployed individuals, have shown improvements in digital skills and job prospects. These success stories underscore the importance of targeted and sustainable interventions, demonstrating that the digital divide can be addressed through effective planning and implementation.

TECHNOLOGY AND PRIVACY BALANCING INNOVATION AND PERSONAL FREEDOM

The previous section highlighted the significant societal challenge of the digital divide, emphasizing the inequalities stemming from unequal access to technology and digital literacy.

This disparity, however, is inextricably linked to another crucial issue: the complex interplay between technology and privacy. The rapid advancement of technology, particularly in areas like data analytics, artificial intelligence, and ubiquitous surveillance, presents profound ethical and societal challenges concerning the protection of personal information and individual freedom. We now find ourselves navigating a landscape where the very convenience and interconnectedness offered by technology often come at the cost of our privacy.

This trade-off—innovation versus personal freedom —is not a simple binary choice. Technological progress has undeniably brought about immense benefits, from improved healthcare and communication to greater access to information and education. However, the increasing sophistication of data collection and analysis techniques raises serious concerns. Our digital footprints—the trails of data we leave behind through our online activities—are constantly being collected, analyzed, and used by various entities, often without our full knowledge or consent. This vast accumulation of personal data poses significant risks to individual privacy and autonomy.

The ethical implications are multifaceted. Consider the pervasive nature of data collection. Every online search, every social media post, and every online purchase contribute to a vast database of personal information. This data is often used for targeted advertising, personalized content delivery, and even predictive policing. While personalization can enhance user experience, the underlying mechanisms raise questions about manipulation and the erosion of individual agency. Are we truly making informed choices, or are our decisions subtly shaped by algorithms designed to influence our behavior?

Surveillance technologies further complicate the picture. From facial recognition software to location tracking apps, the potential for constant monitoring is ever-present. While proponents argue that these technologies enhance security and improve public safety, critics point to the potential for abuse, discrimination, and the chilling effect on freedom of expression and association. The use of such technologies necessitates a careful consideration of the balance between security needs and the preservation of fundamental rights. The potential for misuse, particularly by authoritarian regimes, is a significant concern.

The issue extends beyond overt surveillance. The increasing sophistication of data analysis techniques allows for the creation of detailed profiles of individuals, predicting their behavior and preferences with remarkable accuracy. This capacity raises concerns about discrimination, profiling, and the potential for manipulative practices. For instance, algorithms used in loan applications or employment screenings could perpetuate existing biases, leading to unfair outcomes for certain groups. The lack of transparency in these algorithms further exacerbates the problem, making it difficult to identify and rectify these biases.

Current legislation regarding data protection attempts to address these concerns, but the rapid pace of technological change often outstrips the capacity of law to keep up. Regulations like the

General Data Protection Regulation (GDPR) in Europe and the California Consumer Privacy Act (CCPA) in the United States represent significant strides towards greater data protection, granting individuals more control over their personal data and requiring organizations to be more transparent about their data practices. These laws, however, vary considerably across jurisdictions, creating a fragmented and often inconsistent regulatory landscape. The challenges of enforcing these laws across international borders are considerable, particularly in the context of multinational corporations operating globally.

Furthermore, the very definition of privacy is evolving in the digital age. The norms and expectations surrounding privacy in the physical world do not always translate seamlessly to the digital realm. The seemingly casual sharing of personal information online often masks a lack of understanding of the potential consequences. The ease with which data can be collected, stored, and shared makes it crucial to foster a greater awareness of the risks and empower individuals to make informed decisions about their privacy.

Addressing the challenges posed by technology and privacy requires a multi-pronged approach. Technological solutions, such as differential privacy techniques and federated learning, offer promising avenues for enhancing data protection while still enabling valuable data analysis. Differential privacy, for example, adds carefully designed noise to datasets, preserving the aggregate characteristics of the data while protecting the privacy of individual data points. Federated learning allows machine learning models to be trained on decentralized data sources, eliminating the need to centralize sensitive personal information.

Equally important is the need for stronger legal frameworks and regulatory oversight. Legislation needs to adapt to the rapid pace of technological innovation, balancing the need for data protection with the benefits of technological progress. This requires ongoing dialogue between policymakers, technologists, and civil society to ensure that regulations are both effective and proportionate.

Transparency and accountability are key principles that must underpin the development and deployment of data-driven technologies. Users must have clear and accessible information about how their data is being collected, used, and protected.

Education and public awareness campaigns play a crucial role in fostering informed decision-making. Individuals need to be empowered to understand the risks associated with data sharing and to make conscious choices about their online activities. This requires accessible and engaging educational materials that explain the implications of data collection in simple, understandable terms. Critical thinking skills are crucial for navigating the complexities of the digital age, enabling individuals to evaluate online content and identify potential biases.

Finally, ethical considerations should guide the

development and deployment of all technologies. Technologists, researchers, and policymakers have a responsibility to prioritize privacy and individual autonomy in the design and implementation of new technologies. A strong ethical framework can help to ensure that innovation is not at the expense of fundamental human rights and freedoms. This involves actively considering the potential societal impacts of technological advancements and incorporating privacy by design principles throughout the development lifecycle. Ethical considerations shouldn't be an afterthought; they should be integral to the entire process of technological innovation.

The relationship between technology and privacy is a continuous negotiation, a dynamic tension between progress and freedom. Finding a balance requires a concerted effort from individuals, organizations, and governments. By promoting greater transparency, accountability, and ethical considerations, we can strive towards a future where technological innovation enhances human well-being without sacrificing fundamental rights. The ultimate goal is not to stifle progress but to harness its potential while safeguarding the privacy and autonomy that underpin a free and democratic society. The conversation is ongoing, and our collective engagement is essential to shaping a future where technology serves humanity, not the other way around.

THE SPREAD OF MISINFORMATION AND DISINFORMATION: THE CHALLENGES OF COMBATING FAKE NEWS

The preceding discussion of technology and privacy naturally leads us to another significant societal challenge amplified by the digital age: the proliferation of misinformation and disinformation. The internet, a marvel of human ingenuity designed to connect and inform, has paradoxically become a breeding ground for falsehoods, conspiracy theories, and deliberately manipulative narratives. The ease and speed with which information—accurate or otherwise—can be disseminated across global networks poses unprecedented threats to informed decision-making, social cohesion, and democratic processes. This section delves into the mechanics of misinformation spread, examining the strategies employed by those who create and disseminate fake news, and explores potential countermeasures.

In general, the phrase "misinformation" describes the inadvertent dissemination of inaccurate information. Because they lack critical thinking abilities, rely on untrustworthy sources, or just don't grasp the context, people may unintentionally distribute false information. The purposeful production and distribution of misleading material with the intention of misleading is known as "disinformation," on the other hand. This malevolent intent sets disinformation apart from basic misinformation by emphasizing the evil actor's goal, which may include spreading dangerous ideologies, gaining financial advantage, or manipulating politics. The distinction between these two groups might be hazy, and both have frequently equally harmful effects.

Several factors contribute to the rapid spread of misinformation and disinformation online. Firstly, the architecture of social media platforms often prioritizes engagement over accuracy. Algorithms designed to maximize user interaction tend to favor sensational or emotionally charged content, regardless of its veracity. This creates a feedback loop where false narratives, often presented in emotionally resonant ways, gain more visibility and reach a wider audience than factual information, which may be perceived as less engaging. This inherent bias toward virality significantly amplifies the reach of misinformation.

Second, the anonymity of the web and lack of responsibility supply people and organizations with the confidence to disseminate misleading information without worrying about the immediate consequences. The Internet's decentralized structure makes it difficult to trace the source and spread of false information, which makes it hard to hold individuals or groups accountable for the actions they take. Because of the atmosphere of impunity created by this lack of accountability, misleading narratives can proliferate without any real resistance.

Furthermore, echo chambers and filter bubbles amplify the innate biases of both people and communities. Social media algorithms frequently tailor content to users' interests and past actions, resulting in echo chambers where users are mainly exposed to information that supports their own opinions. This strengthens preconceived notions and reduces people's openness to knowledge that contradicts their beliefs, fostering an environment where false information spreads easily and refutations are difficult to overcome. People may consequently become less receptive to different viewpoints and more polarized in their opinions. In online communities, this may result in a lack of critical thinking and a restriction of intellectual discourse.

The techniques used to create and disseminate disinformation are becoming increasingly sophisticated. Deepfakes, synthetic media that uses artificial intelligence to create realistic-looking but entirely fabricated videos or audio recordings, are a particularly concerning example. These can be used to convincingly portray individuals saying or doing things they never actually did, undermining trust and eroding the credibility of legitimate sources.

Moreover, the use of bots and automated accounts to amplify certain messages artificially inflates their visibility and creates a false sense of widespread support. This coordinated spread of misinformation can overwhelm fact-checking efforts and create a chaotic information environment where it becomes difficult to discern truth from falsehood.

Combating misinformation requires a multi-pronged strategy that addresses both the technological and social aspects of the problem. Media literacy education plays a crucial role in equipping individuals with the critical thinking skills needed to evaluate information sources and identify misinformation. This should involve teaching students how to critically assess online content, identify biases, evaluate evidence, and understand the mechanics of information manipulation. The development of critical thinking is crucial to navigate the complexities of online information.

Technological solutions also offer promising avenues for mitigating the spread of misinformation. Fact-checking organizations play a vital role in identifying and debunking false narratives. However, their capacity is often overwhelmed by the sheer volume of misinformation generated online. The development of advanced algorithms capable of automatically identifying and flagging potentially false information could greatly enhance the effectiveness of fact-checking initiatives. These algorithms could be used to identify patterns and characteristics common to misinformation campaigns, such as the use of emotionally charged language, the repetition of unsubstantiated claims, and the presence of coordinated bot activity.

However, the development and implementation of

such algorithms must be approached with caution. There are concerns about the potential for bias in these algorithms and the risk of censorship. The design and deployment of these tools must prioritize transparency, accuracy, and respect for freedom of expression. Collaboration between technologists, fact-checkers, and policymakers is essential to ensure the responsible development and deployment of these technological solutions.

Moreover, platforms themselves bear a significant responsibility in combating the spread of misinformation. Social media companies need to implement stricter policies regarding the removal of false and misleading content and to enhance the transparency of their algorithms. This would allow researchers and the public to better understand how information is ranked and distributed on their platforms, leading to greater accountability and the potential for identifying and addressing biases. While debates continue about the appropriateness of content moderation and the potential for censorship, the platforms' obligation to combat misinformation cannot be ignored. They have the technical capacity and social responsibility to address this.

Beyond technological solutions and platform responsibility, addressing the broader social and political context within which misinformation flourishes is paramount. Promoting civil discourse and creating spaces for respectful dialogue are crucial to countering the divisive effects of misinformation.

Strengthening trust in institutions and fostering media literacy across all segments of society is also crucial for equipping individuals with the tools to critically evaluate information and resist manipulation.

The spread of misinformation and disinformation represents a complex and evolving challenge. There is no single solution, but a coordinated effort encompassing media literacy, technological innovation, platform accountability, and a societal commitment to truth and reasoned discourse is essential to navigating this treacherous information landscape. The fight against fake news is a continuous battle requiring constant vigilance and adaptation. The future of informed democratic participation hinges upon our ability to effectively address this critical challenge. The stakes are high, and the need for comprehensive and innovative solutions is undeniable. The ongoing struggle to combat misinformation and disinformation is not merely a technological problem but a societal one that demands collective action.

TECHNOLOGY AND POLITICAL POLARIZATION: THE ROLE OF SOCIAL MEDIA

The preceding discussion of misinformation highlights a crucial aspect of technology's societal impact: its contribution to increasing political division.

The internet was originally intended to be a means of promoting understanding and uniting people, but in its current form—especially through social media platforms—it has unintentionally produced a climate that is conducive to divisiveness. The complex connection between social media in particular and the growing political division seen around the world is explored in this section.

The architecture of social media platforms plays a pivotal role in this phenomenon. Algorithms designed to maximize user engagement often prioritize content that elicits strong emotional responses, regardless of its accuracy or neutrality. This inherent bias favors sensationalized or outrage-inducing posts, which tend to be more readily shared and amplified within the network.

Consequently, extreme viewpoints and partisan narratives are disproportionately rewarded with visibility, creating a feedback loop that strengthens echo chambers and reinforces existing biases. Users are increasingly presented with information that aligns with their pre-existing beliefs, limiting their exposure to diverse perspectives and hindering the development of nuanced understanding.

Confirmation bias is a typical human tendency that aggravates this algorithmic amplification of political

opinions. People intentionally avoid or reject information that contradicts their own views while naturally seeking out and interpreting information that supports them. Social media algorithms take advantage of this inclination by giving users a personalized feed that supports their viewpoint while excluding them from opposing viewpoints. This fosters an atmosphere in which opposing ideas are rarely discussed, which heightens animosity and intolerance for them.

This echo chamber effect has serious repercussions. A lack of understanding and a heightened sense of hostility between opposing sides characterize the increasingly splintered and bitter political discourse. The advancement of policy talks and cooperative problem-solving is hampered by the decline in the capacity to have productive conversations and identify points of agreement. Furthermore, as was previously said, these echo chambers significantly increase the spread of misinformation and disinformation since they allow erroneous narratives to easily gain momentum and are rarely contested. The acceptance of unsupported statements is strengthened by a lack of exposure to contradicting facts, which further widens societal divides.

The effects are felt in real-world political engagement as well as online encounters. Increased political separation offline frequently results from the elevated levels of polarization seen online, impacting social interactions, voting behavior, and even personal relationships. The potential for democratic processes to operate efficiently is hampered by the decline in the ability to participate in polite discussion and debate.

The impact of social media on escalating political polarization is demonstrated by a number of particular instances from current political events. A good case study is the US presidential election of 2016. A major factor in influencing public opinion and determining the outcome of the election was the dissemination of false and misleading material on social media platforms. By utilizing algorithmic biases and targeted advertising, political campaigns were able to send customized messages that frequently contained inaccurate or misleading information to particular populations.

Beyond particular election cycles, social media's continuous influence on political polarization is demonstrated by the growing polarization of public discourse. Due to users' frequent aggressive interactions and personal attacks, social media platforms have turned into arenas for ideological conflicts. Because of the anonymity provided by online platforms and the absence of accountability systems, some users feel free to act in an offensive or abusive manner without worrying about the consequences. This hostile internet atmosphere weakens confidence in democratic institutions and fuels political divisiveness.

To overcome this obstacle, a diversified strategy is needed. In order to give people the critical thinking abilities necessary to assess material critically and withstand the appeal of biased or deceptive content, media literacy programs are essential. Users can become more adept at navigating the digital world by learning about the workings of social media algorithms and the strategies employed to sway online debate.

Furthermore, social media platforms themselves must take responsibility for mitigating the spread of polarization. This involves implementing more stringent measures to combat misinformation and hate speech while also promoting algorithmic transparency and user accountability. Greater transparency in algorithms could allow users to understand how their newsfeeds are curated and challenge any biases. More robust mechanisms to deal with online abuse and harassment could discourage the toxic behavior that fuels political division.

Beyond technological solutions, broader societal reforms are necessary. Fostering civil discourse and encouraging constructive dialogue are crucial steps toward bridging the political divide. Initiatives that promote empathy, understanding, and respectful communication can help to de-escalate tensions and foster more tolerant interactions.

Finally, the role of policymakers and regulators cannot be overlooked. Appropriate regulations and policies that promote media responsibility, algorithmic transparency, and user protection are vital in shaping a more positive and less polarized online environment. However, these regulations need to be carefully crafted to protect free speech while effectively curbing the spread of misinformation and harmful content.

The complex interplay between technology and political polarization demands a comprehensive and ongoing effort. A combination of media literacy, platform responsibility, societal reforms, and regulatory measures is required to mitigate the negative impacts of social media on political discourse and rebuild trust and understanding within democratic societies. The challenge is significant, but the potential benefits of a more civil and informed political landscape are immense. The future of healthy democracies depends, in no small part, on navigating this complex relationship successfully.

SHAPING A RESPONSIBLE TECHNOLOGICAL FUTURE: ETHICAL CONSIDERATIONS AND POLICY RECOMMENDATIONS

The prior discussion of how technology affects political division emphasizes how urgently a more comprehensive ethical framework regulating its creation and application is needed. Although technology has enormous potential to improve society, if it develops unchecked, it may worsen already-existing disparities and lead to new challenges. This section discusses the moral issues raised by our world's growing technical sophistication and provides policy suggestions to help manage this challenging environment and create a future in which technology advances humankind's interests.

One of the most pressing ethical concerns centers on algorithmic bias. Algorithms, the unseen engines driving many technological systems, are trained on vast datasets that often reflect existing societal biases. This means algorithms can perpetuate and even amplify inequalities based on race, gender, socioeconomic status, and other factors. For example, facial recognition technology has demonstrated a higher error rate for individuals with darker skin tones, raising serious concerns about its use in law enforcement and security applications. Similarly, algorithmic bias in loan applications can disproportionately disadvantage marginalized communities, perpetuating cycles of poverty. Addressing this requires a multi-pronged approach. Developers must adopt more rigorous testing and auditing procedures to identify and mitigate biases in their algorithms. Moreover, greater transparency in algorithmic design is crucial, allowing for independent scrutiny and accountability. This necessitates the establishment of clear guidelines and standards for algorithmic fairness, ensuring that algorithms are not merely technically sound but also ethically responsible. The development of explainable AI (XAI) is a key step in this direction, enabling users to understand the reasoning behind algorithmic decisions and identify potential biases.

Beyond algorithmic bias, concerns exist regarding

data privacy and security. The proliferation of data-driven technologies necessitates robust mechanisms to protect individual privacy and prevent data breaches. The collection, storage, and use of personal data should be subject to strict ethical and legal guidelines, prioritizing user consent and data minimization. This requires not only the strengthening of existing data protection laws but also the development of innovative technologies that enhance data security and privacy. Differential privacy, for example, allows for the analysis of aggregate data while preserving individual anonymity, offering a potential solution to the trade-off between data utility and privacy. Further, promoting a culture of data literacy among the general population is crucial, empowering individuals to make informed decisions about their data and hold organizations accountable for responsible data handling practices.

The impact of technology on employment is another crucial ethical consideration. Automation and artificial intelligence are transforming the job market, potentially displacing workers in various sectors. While technology creates new job opportunities, the transition can be disruptive and challenging for those whose skills become obsolete. Addressing this requires proactive measures such as retraining and reskilling programs, supporting workers in adapting to the changing demands of the job market. Moreover, exploring alternative economic models, such as universal basic income, could provide a safety net for those displaced by automation, ensuring a more equitable distribution of the benefits of technological progress. Investing in education and lifelong learning is paramount, ensuring that individuals possess the skills needed to thrive in an increasingly automated world. Furthermore, policy interventions could focus on incentivizing industries to invest in retraining their workforces and creating job opportunities in emerging technological sectors.

The ethical implications extend beyond individual concerns, encompassing broader societal impacts. The spread of misinformation and disinformation online, already discussed, poses a serious threat to democratic processes and social cohesion.

Combating this requires a concerted effort involving technology companies, media organizations, educators, and policymakers. This includes strengthening fact-checking initiatives, promoting media literacy, and developing technologies that can effectively identify and flag false or misleading information. Furthermore, legislation may be needed to hold social media platforms accountable for the content they host and to encourage the development of more responsible algorithms that prioritize factual information over sensationalized or emotionally charged content. However, such regulations must be carefully calibrated to avoid stifling free speech while effectively addressing the harmful impacts of misinformation.

Another critical area concerns the accessibility and equitable distribution of technology. The digital divide, the gap between those with access to technology and those without, exacerbates existing inequalities, limiting access to education, healthcare, and economic opportunities. Bridging this divide requires investment in infrastructure, affordable internet access, and digital literacy programs, particularly in underserved communities. Policymakers should prioritize initiatives that make technology accessible to all segments of society, ensuring that technological advancements benefit everyone, not just a privileged few. This also involves considering the accessibility needs of individuals with disabilities, ensuring that technology is designed and developed inclusively.

To effectively address these ethical challenges and shape a responsible technological future, a multi-stakeholder approach is essential. Governments play a crucial role in establishing clear ethical guidelines, enacting appropriate legislation, and investing in research and development that prioritizes ethical considerations.

Industry must take responsibility for developing and deploying technologies in an ethical and responsible manner, prioritizing user privacy, data security, and algorithmic fairness. Individuals, too, have a role to play by being informed consumers of technology, demanding transparency and accountability from technology companies, and advocating for policies that promote responsible technological development. Collaboration between government, industry, academia, and civil society is key to fostering a shared understanding of the ethical implications of technology and to developing effective solutions.

Specific policy recommendations include:

Enacting legislation for algorithmic transparency and accountability: This would require companies to provide clear explanations of how their algorithms work and to undergo independent audits to identify and mitigate biases.

Strengthening data protection laws: This involves enhancing user control over their personal data, strengthening data security measures, and establishing stricter penalties for data breaches.

Investing in education and reskilling programs: This would provide workers with the skills needed to adapt to the changing demands of the job market, mitigating the negative impacts of automation.

Exploring alternative economic models: This could involve considering initiatives such as universal basic income to address potential job displacement caused by automation

Promoting media literacy and combating misinformation: This includes supporting fact-checking initiatives, developing technologies for identifying and flagging false information, and promoting critical thinking skills.

Bridging the digital divide: This requires investing

in infrastructure, affordable internet access, and digital literacy programs, particularly in underserved communities.

Establishing ethical review boards for technological innovation: This would involve creating independent bodies to assess the ethical implications of new technologies before their deployment.

Promoting international cooperation on ethical guidelines for technology: This would ensure a globally consistent approach to responsible technological development.

The development and deployment of technology presents a double-edged sword. Its potential to improve lives and solve pressing global challenges is undeniable. However, without careful consideration of its ethical implications, technology can exacerbate inequalities, erode trust, and undermine social cohesion.

By embracing a multi-stakeholder approach and recommendations, we can harness the power of technology for good while mitigating its potential harms, ensuring a future where technology serves humanity's best interests. This requires a continuous and evolving dialogue, adapting our ethical frameworks and policies to keep pace with the rapid advancements in technology.

The journey toward a responsible technological future is ongoing, requiring vigilance, collaboration, and a commitment to ethical principles above all else.

Having examined technology's impacts across personal, social, and societal dimensions, we arrive at perhaps the most crucial question: How do we transform this understanding into practical action? How do we regain control of our technological lives and ensure that digital tools serve our deepest values rather than undermining them? This final chapter provides a framework for reclaiming our agency in the digital age—not by rejecting technology, but by engaging with it mindfully and intentionally. Through practical strategies and sustainable habits, we can cultivate a relationship with technology that enhances our humanity rather than diminishing it.

CHAPTER 9: RECLAIMING OUR AGENCY: A MINDFUL APPROACH TO TECHNOLOGY

DEVELOPING A MINDFUL RELATIONSHIP WITH TECHNOLOGY: STRATEGIES FOR INTENTIONAL USE

Developing a mindful relationship with technology isn't about throwing away our devices; it's about reclaiming our agency and choosing how technology serves us, rather than the other way around. It means moving from passive consumption to active engagement, recognizing the profound influence technology has on our thoughts, feelings, and behaviors.

The first step toward this mindful approach is self-awareness, understanding your current tech habits, and identifying areas for improvement.

Ask yourself: What apps do you use most? How

much time do you spend on each? Do you reach for your phone even when there's no notification? These questions help pinpoint the patterns and triggers driving your digital engagement.

Journaling can be powerful for this process. Take a few minutes daily to record your technology use. Note not just the apps and websites you visited but also your emotional state before, during, and after using them. Were you stressed, bored, or lonely? Did technology help these feelings or make them worse? This reflection helps uncover why you turn to technology, revealing the emotional needs it might be fulfilling or failing to address. For example, you might discover you frequently check social media when anxious, seeking validation or connection. Recognizing this pattern allows you to explore healthier coping mechanisms beyond digital validation.

Once you understand your patterns, you can set intentional boundaries. This might mean time limits for certain apps, using blockers during work hours, or creating tech-free zones in your home, like the bedroom or dining table. Be realistic and gradual—drastically overhauling your tech use overnight will likely lead to frustration and relapse. Start with small, manageable changes, gradually increasing your boundaries as you gain control. For instance, begin by limiting social media to 30 minutes daily, then gradually reduce it to 20 minutes, and so on.

Consider creating tech-free periods throughout your day. This could be a designated "digital detox" hour each evening, where you disconnect from all screens and engage in activities promoting relaxation and rejuvenation. Reading a book, practicing meditation, or spending time outdoors can counteract technology's stimulating effects and restore mental balance. This isn't about judging technology as good or bad but creating a balanced relationship. These tech-free periods offer space to reconnect with yourself and your surroundings, fostering deeper presence and reducing constant digital distraction.

Cultivating mindfulness in tech use goes beyond setting boundaries. It means being consciously aware of how you engage with digital platforms. Before reaching for your phone, ask yourself, "Why am I doing this? What do I hope to achieve?" This simple question interrupts the automatic impulse to check devices and allows a conscious choice about your actions. Are you truly seeking information, connection, or entertainment, or are you filling a void or avoiding an unpleasant emotion? Recognizing the motivations behind your tech use promotes more intentional and fulfilling engagement.

Actively cultivate alternative sources of satisfaction. If you heavily rely on technology for entertainment or social connection, explore other activities that could fulfill those needs. This might include joining a book club, taking up a new hobby, spending more time with loved ones, or volunteering in your community. By enriching your life with non-digital experiences, you reduce reliance on technology for fulfillment, creating a more balanced and meaningful existence. The goal isn't eliminating technology entirely— that's unrealistic in today's interconnected world— but thoughtfully integrating it into your life so it enhances rather than detracts from your overall well-being.

The mindful approach also involves critically evaluating the information you consume online. The internet is a vast ocean of content, much of it unreliable or manipulative. Develop the habit of fact-checking before sharing information and cultivate skepticism toward emotionally charged content or sensationalized headlines. Engage with diverse perspectives, seeking out sources that challenge your preconceived notions. This promotes critical thinking and reduces the likelihood of falling prey to misinformation and echo chambers.

Mindful technology use also requires protecting your mental and emotional well-being. Pay attention to how technology impacts your mood and energy levels. If you consistently feel drained or anxious after using certain apps or websites, consider limiting your exposure. Recognize the signs of technology addiction—withdrawal symptoms when separated from devices, neglecting responsibilities for digital activities, or feeling compulsive about checking notifications. If you suspect you're struggling with technology addiction, seek professional help from therapists specializing in this area.

Another crucial element is digital responsibility.

This means being aware of the potential negative impacts of your online actions, such as cyberbullying, harassment, and spreading misinformation. Make a conscious effort to be respectful and considerate in online interactions. Think before you post, mindful of the potential consequences of your words and actions. Take responsibility for your digital footprint, understanding that your online activities can have real-world repercussions.

Finally, integrate mindfulness practices into your daily technology use. This might mean brief meditation before engaging with digital platforms or taking short breaks for deep breathing exercises. These practices help regulate your nervous system and reduce the risk of technology overuse. Mindful breathing centers you and helps you approach digital interactions with greater presence and awareness. By consciously incorporating mindfulness into daily digital routines, you can cultivate a more balanced and intentional relationship with technology.

This journey requires patience and self-compassion. Relapses are inevitable; the key is viewing them as learning opportunities rather than failures. Be kind to yourself, acknowledge your struggles, and commit yourself to your goals. The path to a more mindful relationship with technology is an ongoing process, a continuous evolution of awareness and intention. By cultivating these habits, you can harness technology's power for good—using it for connection, creativity, and self-discovery—while safeguarding your mental and emotional well-being. Reclaiming your agency in the digital age isn't about denying technology's presence, but consciously shaping its role in your life, ensuring it serves your values and aspirations rather than dictating them.

It's about creating a future where technology empowers rather than overwhelms us.

DIGITAL WELLBEING: PRIORITIZING MENTAL AND PHYSICAL HEALTH

The previous section outlined strategies for cultivating a mindful relationship with technology, focusing on setting boundaries and cultivating awareness. Building upon this foundation, we now turn to the crucial aspect of digital well-being: prioritizing our mental and physical health in the face of constant digital engagement. In an increasingly interconnected world, technology's influence extends far beyond mere convenience; it deeply impacts our stress levels, sleep patterns, and overall work-life balance. Understanding these impacts and implementing proactive strategies is paramount to maintaining a healthy and fulfilling life.

One of the most significant ways technology affects our well-being is through its contribution to chronic stress. The constant influx of notifications, emails, and social media updates creates a sense of perpetual urgency and pressure.

This "always-on" culture, where we're expected to be instantly responsive, fosters a state of heightened alertness that can lead to burnout and anxiety. Our brains, designed for periods of focused attention interspersed with rest, struggle to cope with the relentless stimulation of the digital world. The dopamine hits associated with social media engagement and notifications, while initially pleasurable, can lead to a dependence that further exacerbates stress when unmet. This constant craving for stimulation can disrupt our natural sleep-wake cycle, reducing restorative sleep and increasing fatigue.

To mitigate the stress-inducing effects of technology, several strategies can be implemented. Firstly, it's crucial to establish clear boundaries between work and personal life. This might involve setting specific times to check work emails, turning off notifications during designated personal time, or creating a dedicated workspace separate from relaxation areas. The goal is to create a mental space where technology doesn't dominate your thoughts, allowing for genuine relaxation and rejuvenation. This separation can be greatly enhanced by physical actions—for example, placing your phone in another room during evenings or creating a designated "technology-free" zone in your home, perhaps your bedroom.

Secondly, mindful practices can play a significant role in stress reduction. Incorporating mindfulness meditation, even for short periods throughout the day, can help regulate the nervous system and improve resilience to stress. Focusing on your breath and cultivating present-moment awareness can counteract the effects of constant digital stimulation, promoting a sense of calm and composure. Mindfulness apps offer guided meditations tailored to different needs and preferences, making this practice accessible to a wide audience. Combining mindfulness with regular physical activity—yoga, running, or even a brisk walk—can further amplify its stress-reducing benefits. Physical exercise not only releases endorphins but also helps to regulate the cortisol response associated with stress.

Another critical aspect of digital well-being is sleep quality.

The blue light emitted from screens interferes with melatonin production, a hormone essential for regulating the sleep-wake cycle. Excessive screen time before bed can lead to sleep disturbances, resulting in daytime fatigue, reduced cognitive function, and increased irritability. To improve sleep quality, it's vital to establish a consistent sleep schedule, create a relaxing bedtime routine, and minimize screen time at least an hour before going to bed. Consider using blue light filtering glasses or apps that adjust screen brightness and color temperature to reduce the impact of blue light.

Creating a calm and dark sleep environment, free from technological distractions, is also crucial for optimal sleep. Consistent sleep patterns are key; our bodies thrive on regularity. The pursuit of a healthy work-life balance is also significantly impacted by technology. The ever-present connectivity fostered by smartphones and laptops can blur the lines between work and personal life, leading to overwork, burnout, and a reduced sense of personal time. To achieve a better work-life balance, it's essential to establish clear boundaries, prioritize tasks effectively, and schedule regular breaks throughout the workday.

Utilizing time management techniques, such as the Pomodoro Technique, can enhance productivity and minimize feelings of being overwhelmed. This technique involves working in focused bursts of 25 minutes, followed by a short 5-minute break. These breaks are crucial for preventing burnout and maintaining focus. Furthermore, it is important to proactively schedule downtime and actively engage in activities that foster relaxation and personal fulfillment. This could involve pursuing hobbies, spending time with loved ones, or simply engaging in activities that bring you joy and a sense of calm.

Beyond stress, sleep, and work-life balance, technology's impact on physical health shouldn't be overlooked. Prolonged sitting, often associated with extensive technology use, can lead to physical health problems such as back pain, neck pain, and eye strain. To mitigate these risks, it's vital to take regular breaks from sedentary activities, ensuring regular physical activity and maintaining good posture. Regular stretching exercises can help alleviate muscle tension caused by prolonged sitting. Integrating physical activity into your daily routine can significantly improve your physical well-being and energy levels. Even short bursts of activity throughout the day, such as taking the stairs instead of the elevator, can make a difference. The key is to incorporate movement regularly rather than engaging in sporadic intense exercise sessions.

Beyond the physical, technology can negatively affect our mental health through social comparison. Social media often presents curated versions of reality, leading to feelings of inadequacy and low self-esteem. Consciously limiting exposure to these platforms and focusing on positive self-talk can help counteract these negative effects. Cultivating a sense of self-compassion and focusing on one's own strengths and accomplishments, rather than constantly comparing oneself to others, is essential for maintaining a positive self-image.

Furthermore, the constant stream of information online can lead to information overload, cognitive fatigue, and a decreased ability to focus. To combat this, it's essential to curate your digital intake carefully, prioritizing reliable sources and limiting exposure to distracting or overwhelming information. Regularly engaging in activities that promote cognitive rest, such as reading a book, listening to music, or spending time in nature, can help improve focus and mental clarity. Our minds, like our bodies, need periods of rest and recovery to function optimally. Creating space in your daily routine for these activities is crucial for maintaining mental well-being.

Finally, a holistic approach to digital well-being involves actively seeking support when needed. If you're struggling to manage your technology use or are experiencing negative impacts on your mental or physical health, don't hesitate to seek professional help.

Therapists and counselors can provide guidance and support in developing healthier habits and coping mechanisms. Recognizing the need for support is a sign of strength, not weakness. Building a support network of friends, family, or professionals can provide valuable assistance during challenging times.

Remember, taking care of your well-being is not a luxury but a necessity. In an increasingly technology-driven world, prioritizing your mental and physical health is crucial for navigating the digital landscape successfully. The mindful approach to technology is not merely about managing our digital lives; it's about ensuring technology enhances our overall well-being rather than hindering it.

While our individual relationship with technology profoundly impacts our personal wellbeing, we must also recognize that these technologies shape entire societies and institutions. The digital revolution extends far beyond personal devices to transform economies, political systems, and social structures. As we've developed strategies to protect our individual mental health, we must now widen our lens to examine how technology creates both opportunities and challenges at the societal level—from access disparities to privacy concerns to the spread of misinformation. Understanding these broader impacts is essential for creating a technological future that serves humanity's collective good.

CULTIVATING DIGITAL LITERACY, CRITICAL THINKING, AND INFORMATION EVALUATION

Building upon the foundation of mindful technology use and its impact on our well-being, we now turn our attention to a critical skill for navigating the digital age: digital literacy. This isn't simply about knowing how to use technology; it's about possessing the critical thinking skills and information evaluation abilities necessary to engage with the online world safely and effectively. In an era saturated with information—much of it unreliable, biased, or outright false—developing strong digital literacy is no longer a luxury but a necessity for informed participation in society.

The sheer volume of information available online presents an unprecedented challenge. While the internet offers unparalleled access to knowledge and diverse perspectives, it also serves as a breeding ground for misinformation and disinformation. We are constantly bombarded with news articles, social media posts, and online advertisements, each vying for our attention and attempting to shape our opinions. Discerning truth from falsehood, fact from opinion, and credible sources from unreliable ones requires a sophisticated level of critical thinking that traditional education systems may not adequately prepare us for.

One of the first steps in cultivating digital literacy is understanding the motivations behind the information we encounter. Not all online content is created equally. Some websites and social media accounts are driven by a genuine desire to inform and educate, while others have ulterior motives. Commercial interests, political agendas, or even malicious actors can manipulate information to sway public opinion, promote specific products, or spread harmful narratives. Becoming aware of these potential biases is crucial to evaluating the credibility of any source.

Consider, for example, an article promoting a particular health supplement. A critical thinker will examine the source of the article. Is it published on a reputable medical journal's website or a blog with undisclosed affiliations? Does the article cite credible scientific studies, or does it rely on anecdotal evidence and unsubstantiated claims? Is there transparency regarding potential conflicts of interest, such as financial ties between the authors and the supplement manufacturer? These are essential questions to ask when evaluating the reliability of health-related information online.

The same rigorous approach should be applied to any type of information, regardless of the topic. Political commentary, news reports, and even seemingly innocuous social media posts should all be subject to the same level of scrutiny.

Furthermore, understanding the concept of confirmation bias is essential for developing critical thinking skills in the digital age.

Confirmation bias is our tendency to favor information that confirms our pre-existing beliefs while ignoring information that challenges them. This cognitive bias can lead us to selectively consume online content that reinforces our viewpoints, creating echo chambers that limit exposure to diverse perspectives and prevent us from engaging in constructive dialogue. To combat this, it's crucial to actively seek out diverse sources of information, particularly those that offer opposing viewpoints. This doesn't necessarily mean accepting everything we read, but it does require us to engage with different perspectives in a thoughtful and unbiased manner.

Developing the ability to identify logical fallacies is another critical component of digital literacy. Logical fallacies are flaws in reasoning that can render an argument invalid. These can range from appeals to emotion or authority to straw man arguments and ad hominem attacks. Recognizing these fallacies is crucial for evaluating the strength and validity of online arguments and distinguishing between persuasive rhetoric and sound reasoning.

For instance, an appeal to authority, while sometimes valid, is a fallacy when the authority cited lacks expertise on the topic in question. Similarly, an ad hominem attack, which focuses on attacking the person making the argument rather than the argument itself, is a fallacy that should be identified and dismissed.

Evaluating the credibility of sources requires a multifaceted approach. Beyond identifying potential biases and logical fallacies, we need to assess the source's expertise, reputation, and track record. Does the source have a history of accuracy and reliability?

Has it been fact-checked by independent organizations? Does the source cite its sources transparently, allowing for verification of information? Are there multiple sources corroborating the information presented? When evaluating websites, look for signs of professionalism, such as a clearly defined "about us" section and contact information. Be wary of websites with poor grammar, outdated information, or a lack of transparency.

In the context of social media, the challenge of evaluating information is further amplified. Social media platforms often prioritize engagement over accuracy, resulting in the rapid spread of misinformation and the amplification of biases. The algorithms used by these platforms can create filter bubbles and echo chambers, limiting exposure to diverse perspectives and reinforcing pre-existing beliefs. Therefore, it's crucial to be discerning about the information we consume on social media and to critically assess the source's credibility before sharing or engaging with it.

Beyond evaluating individual sources, understanding the broader information ecosystem is also critical. The online landscape is complex, with a wide range of actors involved in creating, distributing, and manipulating information. Recognizing the roles of different players—including media outlets, social media platforms, search engines, and individual users —helps us to understand how information flows and the potential biases that might be introduced at each stage. The algorithms that govern social media feeds, for instance, significantly influence which information we see and, consequently, the biases we may be exposed to. Understanding how these algorithms work is crucial for engaging in mindful and critically informed interaction.

Developing digital literacy is an ongoing process, not a one-time achievement. It requires consistent effort and a commitment to critical thinking and information evaluation. Staying informed about current events and emerging trends in the digital world is crucial for adapting to the constantly evolving information landscape. Engaging with reliable sources of information, such as fact-checking websites and reputable news outlets, helps build a strong foundation for critical thinking.

It is also important to understand the techniques used to spread misinformation. These tactics can range from creating fabricated stories and manipulating images and videos to employing sophisticated bots and automated accounts to spread false narratives on a large scale. Recognizing these methods allows us to approach online information with a healthy dose of skepticism and to critically evaluate the evidence presented, rather than accepting it at face value. This involves verifying information across multiple reputable sources, looking for inconsistencies, and understanding the context in which the information is presented.

Furthermore, developing strong media literacy skills complements the development of digital literacy. Media literacy involves understanding how media messages are constructed, the underlying ideologies and biases that may be present, and the impact that media consumption can have on individuals and society.

Developing media literacy enables individuals to critically engage with various forms of media, including news reports, documentaries, advertising, and social media, and to interpret these messages within their wider social and cultural contexts.

We can become more informed consumers of online information, better equipped to identify misinformation and navigate the challenges posed by the digital age. This is not simply about avoiding being misled; it's about participating actively and responsibly in an information-rich society, empowered to make informed decisions and contribute meaningfully to the public discourse. The journey towards digital literacy is a continuous process of learning, reflection, and adaptation, vital for reclaiming our agency in an increasingly technological world.

THE IMPORTANCE OF DIGITAL DETOX: DISCONNECTING TO RECONNECT

The pervasiveness of technology in modern life, while offering undeniable benefits, has also brought about a growing awareness of its potential downsides. The constant connectivity, the incessant stream of notifications, and the ever-present allure of social media can lead to a state of chronic overstimulation, impacting our mental well-being and our ability to engage meaningfully with the world around us. This is where the concept of a "digital detox" comes into play—a conscious and intentional disconnection from technology to reconnect with ourselves, our loved ones, and the present moment.

Digital detox isn't about permanently abandoning technology; it's about strategically stepping away from it to gain a renewed perspective and foster a healthier relationship with the digital world. It's about reclaiming agency over our time and attention, rather than allowing algorithms and notifications to dictate our experiences. The benefits of regular digital detox periods are multifaceted and extend beyond simply reducing screen time.

One of the most significant benefits is the improvement in mental health. Constant exposure to social media, with its curated perfection and relentless comparisons, can contribute to feelings of anxiety, depression, and low self-esteem. The pressure to maintain an online persona, to constantly update our status, and to keep up with the seemingly flawless lives of others takes a toll on our mental well-being. Disconnecting from these pressures, even for a short period, allows us to quiet the internal noise and cultivate a sense of calm and self-acceptance. This reduced exposure allows the mind to rest and recover from the constant barrage of information and stimuli it typically receives. This reduced stimulation can lead to improved sleep quality, reduced stress levels, and a greater sense of mental clarity.

Furthermore, digital detoxes can significantly enhance our interpersonal relationships. When we are constantly glued to our screens, we often neglect the real-life connections that are vital for our happiness and well-being. Face-to-face interactions, meaningful conversations, and shared experiences are often sidelined in favor of online engagement. By intentionally disconnecting, we create space for more genuine interactions, allowing us to strengthen bonds with family and friends and foster a deeper sense of community. The quality of our relationships can be greatly improved through dedicated time spent in meaningful conversation and shared activities, free from the distractions of technology. We reconnect with the nonverbal cues and subtle nuances of human interaction often missed during digital exchanges.

The impact on our attention spans is another crucial aspect of the benefits of digital detox. The constant switching between apps, notifications, and online content fragments our attention, making it harder to concentrate on tasks that require sustained focus. Digital detoxes allow our minds to regain their ability to concentrate, enhancing productivity and cognitive function. This improved focus translates to enhanced performance in various aspects of life, from work and study to creative pursuits and hobbies. The ability to sustain attention is a valuable skill in a world increasingly saturated with distractions.

Beyond the immediate mental health benefits, regular digital detoxes can lead to a greater appreciation for the offline world. We begin to notice the small things—the beauty of nature, the joy of a simple conversation, the satisfaction of a completed task unrelated to a screen. This shift in perspective can foster a deeper sense of gratitude and contentment, enriching our overall experience of life. We rediscover the simple pleasures and activities that might have been overlooked in our technologically driven routines. This can lead to greater self-awareness and a more fulfilling life outside of the digital realm.

Implementing a digital detox effectively requires planning and intentionality. It's not a one-size-fits-all approach; the ideal detox will vary depending on individual needs and preferences. Some may opt for a complete digital disconnect for a weekend, while others might choose shorter, more frequent breaks throughout the week. The key is to find a rhythm that works for you and to commit to it.

One effective technique is to schedule specific "digital-free" times each day. This could be an hour before bed, an hour during lunch, or a specific period in the evening. During these times, engage in activities that promote relaxation and well-being, such as reading, spending time in nature, exercising, or engaging in creative pursuits. This gradual reduction in screen time allows for a smoother transition and makes the detox process more manageable.

Another helpful approach is to establish designated "technology-free zones" in your home. The bedroom, for instance, is an ideal location to minimize technology use, creating a space for restful sleep and disconnecting from the constant stimulation of the digital world. This allows for improved sleep quality and reduces the potential for nighttime screen time disrupting sleep patterns. A designated "technology-free" area in the home provides a haven from digital distractions and promotes a more peaceful environment.

For more intensive detoxes, consider a complete

digital break for a day or a weekend. This requires advance planning, such as informing close contacts of your unavailability and turning off notifications on your devices. During this time, focus on activities that promote relaxation, self-care, and connection with the physical world. Nature walks, spending time with loved ones, or pursuing hobbies are all excellent choices. This intentional disconnection allows a much-needed reset from the constant demands of the digital world.

Choosing specific activities during your digital detox is crucial to its success. Engaging in activities that promote mindfulness and self-reflection can amplify the benefits of disconnecting. Mindfulness practices such as meditation or yoga help cultivate present-moment awareness, reducing stress and promoting a sense of inner peace. Engaging in creative pursuits such as writing, painting, or playing music can provide an outlet for self-expression and a sense of accomplishment, replacing the often superficial satisfaction derived from online interactions. Physical activity, such as going for a walk or run, provides a valuable opportunity to connect with nature and reduce stress levels. Spending quality time with loved ones, free from the distractions of technology, fosters deeper connections and strengthens relationships.

However, a digital detox shouldn't be viewed as a punishment or deprivation. It should be approached as an opportunity for self-discovery and enhanced well-being. This positive framing helps prevent feelings of resentment towards the detox process and fosters a more supportive and successful approach to implementing this important practice. The key is to approach the detox with a positive attitude and view it as a chance to explore new activities and reconnect with yourself and your environment.

The balance between online and offline experiences is crucial. Technology offers many benefits, and completely abandoning it is neither necessary nor desirable for most people. The goal of a digital detox isn't to eliminate technology from your life entirely but to create a more mindful and balanced relationship with it. By incorporating regular digital detoxes into your routine, you can enjoy the benefits of technology while safeguarding your mental and emotional well-being and cultivating a richer, more meaningful life. The digital detox becomes a tool for self-regulation and mindful engagement with technology, not an eradication of it.

The practice of regular digital detoxes is a crucial skill for navigating the complexities of the digital age. By intentionally disconnecting from technology, we reclaim agency over our time and attention, cultivate healthier mental well-being, and foster deeper connections with ourselves and others. It's an empowering act of self-care, leading to a more balanced and fulfilling life. This mindful approach to technology allows us to harness the benefits of digital innovation while mitigating its potentially harmful effects, creating a sustainable and enriching relationship with the ever-evolving digital landscape. The journey towards a healthier relationship with technology begins with a conscious decision to disconnect—to pause, reflect, and reconnect with what truly matters.

EMBRACING TECHNOLOGICAL PROGRESS RESPONSIBLY: A CALL TO ACTION

Embracing technological progress responsibly requires a fundamental shift in our relationship with technology. It's not about rejecting innovation but about cultivating a mindful and intentional approach to its use. We've explored the profound psychological impact of technology, from the addictive nature of social media to the subtle manipulation of algorithms. We've dissected the ways in which constant connectivity affects our attention spans, memory, and even our capacity for empathy. This understanding forms the basis for a responsible engagement with the digital world.

The first step is self-awareness. Understanding how technology affects us individually is paramount. We must be cognizant of our own digital habits—how much time we spend online, which platforms we use most, and how these platforms impact our moods and behaviors. Tracking our screen time, for instance, can provide valuable insights into our usage patterns, allowing us to identify areas where we might need to make adjustments. This self-reflection is crucial for establishing a more balanced relationship with technology.

Furthermore, it's vital to recognize the subtle ways in which technology shapes our perceptions and choices. Algorithms are designed to maximize engagement, often at the expense of our well-being.

Understanding these mechanisms allows us to navigate the digital landscape more critically, recognizing when we're being manipulated or nudged towards specific behaviors. We need to be conscious consumers of digital content, questioning the sources of information and the motivations behind the platforms we use.

Developing digital literacy is another critical aspect of responsible technology engagement. This encompasses not only technical skills but also a critical understanding of the social, political, and ethical implications of technology. We need to be able to critically evaluate the information we encounter online, discern credible sources from misinformation, and understand the potential biases embedded within algorithms and data sets. This heightened awareness empowers us to navigate the digital world with greater discernment and resilience.

Beyond individual responsibility lies the need for collective action.

We need to advocate for policies that protect users' privacy, promote digital well-being, and address the ethical challenges posed by artificial intelligence and big data. This requires engaging in public discourse, supporting organizations working to promote digital responsibility, and demanding accountability from technology companies. We must hold these companies responsible for the impact of their products on individuals and society.

This involves supporting research that explores the long-term effects of technology on human behavior and well-being. Funding initiatives that investigate the societal impact of AI, the development of ethical guidelines for algorithmic design, and the creation of effective interventions to mitigate the negative consequences of technology are crucial. The collaborative effort of researchers, policymakers, and technology developers is vital in shaping a future where technology serves humanity, rather than the other way around.

The development of digital ethics is another area requiring collective attention. This involves establishing clear guidelines and principles for the design, development, and deployment of technology. It necessitates a thoughtful consideration of the ethical implications of emerging technologies, particularly in areas such as artificial intelligence, data privacy, and automation. These guidelines must prioritize human well-being, fairness, transparency, and accountability. The creation of interdisciplinary forums that bring together technologists, ethicists, social scientists, and policymakers is vital in this effort.

Education plays a critical role in shaping a responsible relationship with technology. This isn't just about teaching technical skills; it's about cultivating critical thinking, media literacy, and a sense of digital citizenship. From primary school to higher education, we need curricula that equip individuals with the knowledge and skills to navigate the complexities of the digital age responsibly. This includes teaching students how to critically evaluate online information, understand the ethical implications of technology, and engage in constructive dialogue about its societal impact.

In addition to formal education, informal learning initiatives are also crucial. Workshops, online courses, and public awareness campaigns can educate individuals about the potential benefits and risks of technology and promote responsible digital practices. These initiatives should focus on empowering individuals to make informed choices about their technology use and engage in constructive dialogue about the future of technology.

Furthermore, fostering a culture of mindful technology use requires promoting alternative perspectives and practices. This includes encouraging digital minimalism, emphasizing the value of offline experiences, and celebrating the richness of human connection. We need to counter the dominant narrative that equates constant connectivity with productivity and happiness. Instead, we need to cultivate a more balanced and nuanced understanding of technology's role in our lives.

The transition to a more responsible relationship with technology requires a paradigm shift—a move from passive consumption to active engagement. We are not mere consumers of technology; we are its creators, its users, and its ultimate shapers. We have the power to demand better, to advocate for change, and to build a future where technology truly serves humanity's best interests. This requires individual responsibility, collective action, and a sustained commitment to creating a more humane and equitable digital world.

Ultimately, reclaiming our agency in the digital age is about more than just managing our screen time or limiting our social media use.

It's about cultivating a deep understanding of how technology shapes our thoughts, feelings, and behaviors. It's about developing critical thinking skills, engaging in informed discussions, and advocating for a more responsible and equitable technological landscape. It's about creating a future where technology empowers us, rather than controlling us.

This mindful approach is not a temporary fix but a fundamental shift in our relationship with technology—a commitment to a more balanced, purposeful, and human-centered future.

The journey of responsible technology engagement is a continuous process of learning, adaptation, and collective action, requiring constant vigilance and a commitment to prioritizing human values and well-being above all else. Only through this mindful engagement can we truly harness the transformative potential of technology while mitigating its inherent risks.

The future of our relationship with technology is not predetermined; it is a future we create together

REFERENCES AND SOURCES

ACADEMIC RESEARCH

Alter, Adam. (2017). *Irresistible: The Rise of Addictive Technology and the Business of Keeping Us Hooked.* Penguin Press.

Anderson, M., & Jiang, J. (2018). "Teens, Social Media & Technology 2018." Pew Research Center.

Bauer, A. A., Loy, L. S., Masur, P. K., & Schneider, Г. M. (2021). "Mindful use of digital media – An intervention study." Journal of Media Psychology, 33(1), 4-15.

Brailovskaia, J., & Margraf, J. (2020). "Relationship between depression symptoms, physical activity, and addictive social media use." Cyberpsychology, Behavior, and Social Networking, 23(11), 818-822.

Carr, Nicholas. (2010). *The Shallows: What the Internet Is Doing to Our Brains.* W. W. Norton & Company.

Cho, J. (2022). "Digital well-being matters: The impact of digital media use on psychological well-being."

Current Opinion in Psychology, 45, 101313.

Eyal, Nir. (2019). *Indistractable: How to Control Your Attention and Choose Your Life*. BenBella Books.

Firth, J., Torous, J., Stubbs, B., Firth, J. A., Steiner, G. Z., Smith, L., Alvarez-Jimenez, M., Gleeson, J., Vancampfort, D., Armitage, C. J., & Sarris, J. (2019). "The 'online brain': How the Internet may be changing our cognition." World Psychiatry, 18(2), 119-129.

Harris, Tristan. (2020). "How Technology Hijacks People's Minds — from a Magician and Google's Design Ethicist." Center for Humane Technology.

He, Q., Turel, O., & Bechara, A. (2017). "Brain anatomy alterations associated with social networking site addiction." Scientific Reports, 7(1), 45064.

Kushlev, K., & Dunn, E. W. (2019). "Smartphones distract parents from cultivating feelings of connection when spending time with their children." Journal of Social and Personal Relationships, 36(6), 1619-1639.

Lorenz-Spreen, P., Mønsted, B. M., Hövel, P., & Lehmann, S. (2019). "Accelerating dynamics of collective attention." Nature Communications, 10(1), 1759.

McDaniel, B. T., & Coyne, S. M. (2016). "'Technoference': The interference of technology in couple relationships and implications for women's personal and relational well-being." Psychology of

Popular Media Culture, 5(1), 85-98.

Newport, Cal. (2019). *Digital Minimalism: Choosing a Focused Life in a Noisy World.* Portfolio.

Pariser, Eli. (2011). *The Filter Bubble: What the Internet Is Hiding from You.* Penguin Press.

Przybylski, A. K., & Weinstein, N. (2017). "A large-scale test of the Goldilocks Hypothesis: Quantifying the relations between digital-screen use and the mental well-being of adolescents." Psychological Science, 28(2), 204-215.

Sanbonmatsu, D. M., Strayer, D. L., Medeiros-Ward, N., & Watson, J. M. (2013). "Who multi-tasks and why? Multi-tasking ability, perceived multi-tasking ability, impulsivity, and sensation seeking." PLOS ONE, 8(1), e54402.

Sunstein, Cass R. (2017). *#Republic: Divided Democracy in the Age of Social Media.* Princeton University Press.

Twenge, J. M., Joiner, T. E., Rogers, M. L., & Martin, G. N. (2018). "Increases in depressive symptoms, suicide-related outcomes, and suicide rates among U.S. adolescents after 2010 and links to increased new media screen time." Clinical Psychological Science, 6(1), 3-17.

Vosoughi, S., Roy, D., & Aral, S. (2018). "The spread of true and false news online." Science, 359(6380), 1146-1151.

Ward, A. F., Duke, K., Gneezy, A., & Bos, M. W.

(2017). "Brain drain: The mere presence of one's own smartphone reduces available cognitive capacity." Journal of the Association for Consumer Research, 2(2), 140-154.

Wilmer, H. H., Sherman, L. E., & Chein, J. M. (2017). "Smartphones and cognition: A review of research exploring the links between mobile technology habits and cognitive functioning." Frontiers in Psychology, 8, 605.

Zuboff, Shoshana. (2019). *The Age of Surveillance Capitalism: The Fight for a Human Future at the New Frontier of Power*. PublicAffairs.

Dunbar, Robin I.M. (2016). "Do online social media cut through the constraints that limit the size of offline social networks?" *Royal Society Open Science*, 3(1).

McDaniel, Brandon T., & Coyne, Sarah M. (2016). "'Technoference': The interference of technology in couple relationships and implications for women's personal and relational well-being." Psychology of Popular Media Culture, 5(1), 85-98.

Roberts, James A., & David, Meredith E. (2016). "My life has become a major distraction from my cell phone: Partner phubbing and relationship satisfaction among romantic partners." *Computers in Human Behavior*, 54, 134-141.

Przybylski, Andrew K., & Weinstein, Netta (2013). "Can you connect with me now? How the presence of mobile communication technology influences face-to-face conversation quality." *Journal of Social and Personal Relationships*, 30(3), 237-246.

Sbarra, David A., Briskin, Julia L., & Slatcher, Richard B. (2019). "Smartphones and Close Relationships: The Case for an Evolutionary Mismatch." *Perspectives on Psychological Science*, 14(4), 596-618.

D'Angelo, Jonathan & Toma, Catalina L. (2017). "There Are Plenty of Fish in the Sea: The Effects of Choice Overload and Reversibility on Online Daters' Satisfaction With Selected Partners." *Media Psychology*, 20(1), 1-27.

INTERVIEWS AND EXPERT SOURCES

Dr. Adam Alter, Professor of Marketing at New York University's Stern School of Business and author of "Irresistible"

Dr. Anna Lembke, Chief of the Stanford Addiction Medicine Dual Diagnosis Clinic and author of "Dopamine Nation"

Dr. BJ Fogg, Director of the Stanford Behavior Design Lab

Dr. Jean Twenge, Professor of Psychology at San Diego State University and author of "iGen"

Dr. Larry Rosen, Professor Emeritus of Psychology at California State University, Dominguez Hills

Linda Stone, former Apple and Microsoft executive who coined the term "continuous partial attention"

Jaron Lanier, computer scientist and author of "Ten Arguments for Deleting Your Social Media Accounts Right Now"

Tristan Harris, former Google Design Ethicist and co-founder of the Center for Humane Technology

Dr. Sherry Turkle, Professor of the Social Studies of Science and Technology at MIT and author of "Alone Together" and "Reclaiming Conversation"

DATA SOURCES AND REPORTS

Common Sense Media. (2021). "The Common Sense Census: Media Use by Tweens and Teens."

GlobalWebIndex. (2023). "Digital 2023: Global Digital Overview."

Pew Research Center. (2021). "Social Media Use in 2021."

World Health Organization. (2019). "Guidelines on physical activity, sedentary behaviour and sleep for children under 5 years of age."

Pew Research Center (2022). "Parenting Children in the Age of Screens."

Pew Research Center (2020). "Americans' Views on Mobile Etiquette."

Massachusetts Institute of Technology - Social Physics Research (2018). "Digital versus In-person Interaction Study."

MEDIA ARTICLES AND OTHER SOURCES

"The Attention Economy: How Tech Companies Compete for Your Time." The Economist, August 2017.

"Have Smartphones Destroyed a Generation?" The Atlantic, September 2017 issue.

"Your Smartphone Reduces Your Brainpower, Even If It's Just Sitting There." Harvard Business Review, March 20, 2018.

"The Social Dilemma" (2020). Documentary film directed by Jeff Orlowski.

"Design tech to build awareness of emotional health." National Academies of Sciences, Engineering, and Medicine workshop summary, 2018.